D0930234

LESSONS FROM A DESPERADO POET

Also by Baxter Black

LESSONS FROM A DESPERADO POET

HOW to Find Your Way When You Don't Have a Map, **HOW** to Win the Game **WHEN** You Don't Know the Rules, and When Someone Says It Can't Be Done, **WHAT** They Really Mean Is *They* Can't Do It.

BAXTER BLACK

TWODOT®

GUILFORD, CONNECTICUT
HELENA, MONTANA

AN IMPRINT OF GLOBE PEQUOT PRESS

To buy books in quantity for corporate use
or incentives, call **(800) 962-0973**
or e-mail **premiums@GlobePequot.com**.

A · **T W O D O T**® · **B O O K**

All photos courtesy of Coyote Cowboy Company unless otherwise noted.

Text design: Sheryl Pirolo Kober
Layout: Maggie Peterson
Project editor: Kristen Mellitt

Library of Congress Cataloging-in-Publication Data is available on file.

ISBN 978-0-7627-6997-1

Printed in the United States of America

10 9 8 7 6 5 4 3 2 1

CONTENTS

SECTION ONE—HOW I LEARNED:

Through early entrepreneurial ventures,
Through wrestling with implanted but disorganized values,
And through dealing with the fear of losing a regular paycheck.

SECTION TWO—WHAT I LEARNED:

To depend on my marketing ability to survive,
To think outside the box,
And to appreciate the importance of integrity.

SECTION THREE—WHY I WAS ABLE TO LEARN:
By maintaining my inner values,
By trusting my intuitions,
And by developing a faith that transcends publicity.

FOREWORD
BY WILFORD BRIMLEY

In the first chapter of this book, I was immediately taken back to a period in my life when Baxter Black and I trod the same ground. He credits John Basabe as the inspiration for his title. I knew John. He was a tough, hardheaded Basco who managed the farm, feedlot, and ranch divisions of the Simplot Livestock Company headquartered in Grand View, Idaho.

John was one of the Big Dogs in that Snake River and sagebrush country where agriculture was king. He was one of those "men of consequence," who traded on a handshake, moved mountains, and never forgot the foot soldiers who laid the track on which he rode.

Baxter was the young DVM for the Simplot Livestock Company. I was a horseshoer. My clients included many of the operations run by men like John Basabe, such as Jim and Terry Roeser, Jack, Joe, and their dad Harold Doan, Bill Richardson, Henry Rubelt, Chuck and Doris Tyson, Theron Adcock, Milt Corothers, Walt Love, and Henry Hatton.

These men and women practiced the "Cowboy Way." They survived on their wits, on bravado, and on bonds formed in the fire of adversity. They also taught pups like Baxter and me. Not with PowerPoint presentations, lengthy written reports, or windy seminars, but by example. They left us deep tracks to follow.

They didn't draw a map, but they showed me how to find my way without one. When I was shoein' horses at the feedlot in Caldwell, Idaho, I don't think anyone would have bet on me to be in the same state as Paul Newman, much less the same room! I'm not sure if there is one way that works for everyone. Each has to find his own compass. I learned by example, both good and bad, and kept workin' till one day I looked up and found myself sittin' here writing a foreword to a book!

If my dad was still around, I'd have to look at him and say, "Hell, Dad, I don't believe it either!"

Maybe if I'd had the guidelines in Baxter's book to go by, who knows . . . I might have gone ahead and finished the eighth grade!

Humor, common sense, and wisdom that comes only through experience and keeping your eye on the road . . . that's what this book is about to me.

Wilford Brimley was raised in Utah, served in the U.S. Marines, trained and shod horses, and went to Hollywood in the '60s as a cowboy stuntman. This led him to acting and eventually to parts in hundreds of movies and television shows such as True Grit, The China Syndrome, The Electric Horseman, Absence of Malice, The Thing, Cocoon, The Firm, *and* The Natural, *as well as spokesman positions for Quaker Oats and Liberty Medical.*

He often plays rugged, salty, no-nonsense characters who aren't above putting a whoopee cushion in the vice president's chair. About his acting he simply says, "I just try to be myself."

Courtesy of Wilford Brimley

INTRODUCTION

"In your book you say, 'You'll never be able to make a living writing poems.'"

AN EXCERPT FROM AN INTERVIEW BETWEEN TERRY GROSS
OF NPR's FRESH AIR, AND TED KOOSER, AT THE TIME THE
NATION'S REIGNING POET LAUREATE AND PULITZER PRIZE
WINNER FOR POETRY

Baxter Black is . . . "probably the nation's most successful living poet."

NEW YORK TIMES

I worked for a scientist in a veterinary parasitology lab in my youth who told me, "Son, you can't use too much tape." The premise of this book is "You can't shoot too many arrows in the sky." Working outside the system is like shooting at a moving target . . . blindfolded! It does not take a genius; it just requires the persistence of a glacier. Lesson #20 from Chapter 4: Remember, often it is not ability, it's reliability. The world is run by those who show up.

To the reader seeking inspiration and instruction for reaching their own goal, you may find, as I have, it is not the pinnacle itself that matters in the end, but rather what it takes you to get there. This book gives the reader the background that formulated my work ethic, my career as a veterinarian where I developed my confidence, and my climb to a position of modest celebrity as a cowboy poet and an accomplished self-marketer.

There are uncountable self-help, motivational, inspirational, business, love, and peace books in print. But there is only one you, and only one me. There are a million ways to get bucked off, a million love songs, and millions of stars in the sky. But most of us can name at least one constellation, hum one love song, and remember one horse that bucked us off. Each of us is unique.

This book is different from other self-help books because I am different and this is my tale. Those who have purchased my previous books, read my column, listened to me on the radio, seen me at live shows or on television, can hear my voice in these pages. You will be able to picture my gesticulations and pratfalls and watch my occasionally less-than-nimble mind trying to outdo the bad horse, mad cow, or crafty barn cat. If you buy this book, it will put you in the company of people who have never been to a psychologist, seen *Oprah,* or read Joel Osteen! Even people who have never bought a self-help book! It will be most helpful to those who already believe they can help themselves and just need a new idea.

Of course, it will be entertaining! I mean, where else can you walk with someone down the center of I-25 in downtown Denver at midnight? Be admitted to veterinary school even though you flunked calculus and eked out a 1.8 grade point average? Have you ever been officially detained at the John Wayne Airport for molesting a stamp machine?

Allow me to give you a taste of some of the skewed logic and commonsense lessons I have learned that might stir up your curiosity:

You'll be amazed at how capable people think you are if they don't know you well. Don't waste that advantage.

Remember, if you think your book is good, you can always get a second opinion.

Always remember it is the job of the radio programmer, newspaper editor, and book publisher to keep you out of print and off the air. Don't take it personally.

If it takes more than ten minutes to explain how you make a living, you are self-unemployed!

Air travel is the cheapest, safest way to get somewhere. Just don't expect them to treat you like a customer at Ruth's Chris Steak House!

It's not how much you made, it's did they get their money's worth.

CAUGHT IN AN EXAGGERATION!

The clips at the beginning of this introduction, from the *Fresh Air* interview and the *New York Times* quote beneath it, are a thumbnail sketch of the challenge I faced as a self-confessed poet, and the result of my efforts. They represent both my obstacular Mt. Everest and my footprints at the top. It is my equivalent to Gus Grissom's landing on the moon, or Freckles Brown riding Tornado. It's all just part of the job, when you don't know it can't be done.

Thanx for ridin' with me!

SECTION ONE

HOW I LEARNED:

Through early entrepreneurial ventures,

Through wrestling with implanted but disorganized values,

And through dealing with the fear of losing a regular paycheck.

CHAPTER 1
The Basque Infusion

I attribute the title of this book to the lessons I learned working for a hardheaded Basque named John Basabe. He was the general manager of a large livestock operation in the Northwest where I spent ten years of my life.

Courtesy of Tom Basabe

John Basabe

I had begun my cattle business career working as a feedlot hand and later a veterinarian for another large livestock operation in the Southwest. For the most part, then and now, the management philosophy of the Northwest and the Southwest differs. Operations in the Southwest functioned like typical "corporate" businesses. In other words, there was a management chart, a list of objectives, chain of command, job description, regular meetings, grievance hearings, salary grades, and group decisions. One presumes that some effort has been made to appear organized.

Working within the parameters of this type of structure, it would be possible to go to Texas A&M and acquire a degree in feedlot management and be taken seriously! As an employee and "member of the team," you knew what was expected of you and where you stood. It was from this organized work environment that I set out north to work for John.

I stepped knee-deep into another management style I call the Farmer-Feeder operation. This is the type that dominates the Midwest and the Northwest. In John's operation the general manager was the boss. That was him. He reported to one man, the owner. We didn't have meetings. Job descriptions were vague, and crossover responsibility created confusion.

I was hired as the "company veterinarian" for three feedlots with a total of 100,000 capacity, five ranches with 10,000 mother cows, 20,000 sheep, and a new 1,000-cow dairy. The operation covered several states including Idaho, Oregon, Utah, Nevada, and northern California.

First day on the new job I went down to the doctor shack. It was a cold spring morning, and the cowboys had come in for the 9:30 coffee break. I walked in and introduced myself as the new veterinarian. I explained that I hoped we could all work together, learn from each other, and do a better job taking care of the cattle. After I had run out of air, I asked if anybody had any questions. Nobody said a word. Then this ol'-timer, Bud Dacy was his name, rose, dumped the dregs of his cup into the sink, and looked at me. He spoke, "I was punchin' cows before you could drag a halter chain."

Company vet
Simplot Livestock Co.
Idaho

He pulled his hat down and walked out the door . . . followed by the entire cowboy crew.

It was a humbling start.

BUCKIN' OFF O.C.

I had come from a company that employed a consulting nutritionist, had a computerized feeding system, trained the feed boss, produced statistical information to show average daily gain, consumption, conversion, and cost. All of this was necessary if you were custom feeding cattle and needed to bill the customer.

In Idaho we fed potato waste. The company owned all the cattle. They did not deem it necessary to monitor the details. We had a good consulting nutritionist who came monthly, took the boss to town for a three-martini lunch, returned a lot of phone calls, and designed the rations.

My second day on the job, John walked into the newly cleaned-out storeroom that was my office and threw a manila folder on my desk. "Take care of this, too," he said, and left. I opened the folder to find mimeographed sheets containing the three basic feed rations for all the cattle in the feedlots. I was stunned.

He didn't ask me if I had ever taken a class in nutrition (which I hadn't), ever fed potatoes (which I hadn't), or if I could drive a feed truck (which I couldn't)!

Youthful ignorance carried the day. I put aside the fact that where I had come from there was a whole feed department! "Couldn't be that hard," I told myself. If the nutritionist could give me the rations, I could work with the feed boss and mill man to make sure what was on the paper was what came out in the feed bunk. I admit I made a lot of calls to the nutritionist. He usually called back when he was at the next feedlot having lunch with the manager. I'm just thankful he took them!

Several weeks went by. I traveled to all the company feedlots and ranches, establishing veterinary treatment programs and acquainting myself with each feedlot's feed system. I was too busy to be overwhelmed with the responsibility I had been given; i.e., overseeing the health and nutrition of thousands of cattle. I was a bit prideful.

I didn't see John much. He was busy and traveled each week to the company operations, as did I. One Saturday morning I caught him in his office. He was writing, working on something. I interrupted. He looked up. "You need something?" he asked. He seemed preoccupied, but I stumbled on, "Yeah, John, I just wanted to thank you for hirin' me. I think I'm findin' my way around and all. Ya know, with the herd health and rations, but I could do a lot better job, I think, if maybe once a week I could have a short visit with you to make sure I'm on the right track."

His eyes narrowed. He said, "I ain't got time for your piddly problems." He didn't smile.

"Well," I huffed, "well . . . I guess I'll just do what I think's right and if I'm wrong, I reckon you'll tell me."

"Count on it," he said.

I backed out the door. "Freedom's just another word for nothin' left to lose . . . except," I thought, "my job!"

Lesson #3: You can walk a long way toward the horizon before you step off it . . . or in my case, in it. You have to get over the idea that if you do something wrong you will automatically be fired. Truth be known, most of the decisions you make aren't that important anyway!

My saving grace was that I had many good advisors: the cowboys, the mill men, the consulting nutritionist, other feed-lot veterinarians, and various managers of the other company operations. I kept busy and paid attention.

I had been there a year when I got a call on the two-way radio in my pickup. "One to Five."

"This is Five, John, go ahead."

"Are those heifers in pen 14C big enough to breed?"

"Lemme take a look," I said.

"One out."

I knew the heifers in 14C like the back of my hand. I passed them every day on the way to work and looked them over, but it was an odd question so I didn't want to answer lightly. I drove to the pen. They were feedlot heifers destined for the meatpacking plant, so why did he want to know if they were big enough to breed?

"Five to One."

"Go ahead."

"I'm guessing these heifers weigh five-fifty. There's quite a few blacks and black ballys. They mature earlier and they are gaining good, so I'd say a large portion of them will be cycling and probably settle, but they—"

"Breed 'em! One Out."

I drove down to the office to ask John to elaborate. "We've bought two new ranches and we're gonna need lots of replacement cows and heifers."

I didn't ask him how I was to go about this, and he never offered any advice except "Breed 'em! One Out!" I got to work and rented sixty black bulls. We put them right in the big grower pen with the 1,250 heifers and left them for thirty days. We had a 62 percent conception rate!

Lesson #4: If necessity is the mother of invention, then responsibility is the mother of ingenuity. If the buck stops somewhere else, sooner or later it's bound to get passed your way, so be ready!

He led me not to fear making decisions. It is difficult to work for a committee, as any association executive can tell you, because the committee members often disagree, and getting something done can be a gruesome task.

On the simple command, "Breed 'em," John started a complicated, extensive, fairly successful breeding and calving

program that eventually involved over one hundred Washington State Veterinary students, two calving barns, a crew of Basque sheepherders, the cowboys, and me. It consumed thousands of hours, created jillions of lifelong memories, and generated over five thousand cows with calves in the six years that it ran.

John had his own way to solve problems. He saw the big picture, knew the answer, and left us to figure out how to do it. He never doubted it could be done. It was the equivalent of President Kennedy saying, "We're going to land a man on the moon before Russia does, now get with it!"

In the annals of corporate committee management, a solution so simple and drastic would have never been reached.

Lesson #5: Whether it's 8 or 800, you figure out how to do the first one then multiply it by two, or five, or one hundred, or 1,250. Whether it's cows, mail-order solicitations, or moving rocks, all it takes is more help and more room.

Shutterstock

In the ensuing years at his direction, I oversaw or was directly involved in the building of a grain mill, running a feed store, buying grain, buying bulls, managing a dairy, dehydrating potato waste, recycling cow manure, and many other projects that had very little to do with my veterinary education.

When I hear the term "thinking outside of the box," sometimes I wonder if John was *ever* restricted to a box.

Lesson #6: It's not that what he knew stopped him, it's that what he didn't know didn't stop him.

His thinking was not restricted by "too much information." Like inventors, explorers, and artists, he was limited only by his imagination.

I am computer illiterate, by choice. In my office there are five computers all manned by competent people. We have a consulting programmer and a web page person. I find the technology fascinating and miraculous.

I read the articles about technological advances and their purpose, impact, and usefulness. I am occasionally surprised when I ask about an application or service and am told computers can't do that! My thinking is not limited by knowing what they can't do.

My imagination for the computer's capability is not restricted by too much knowledge. I'm free to think beyond the screen. It is literally how to find your way when you don't have a map. How many times have you studied a map for ten minutes before you look up and see Scotts Bluff, the Golden Gate Bridge, or Chesapeake Bay right in front of you?

Lesson #7: Although a poor checkers player can never beat a good checkers player, a poor chess player can beat a good chess player once.

The Basque men played checkers in the sheep camps. *Damas,* they called them. I was never able to beat them. When they played each other, the winner was inevitably the one who made the first move, and he won by one move.

I also play chess. On a vacation to Mexico I ran into a British traveler who played it well. He had just bought a set in a local Mexican curio shop. *Ajedrez* is what it is called.

"Do you play?" he asked me.

"A little," I said.

He set up the board on the hotel veranda. It was not that hard-fought a game. I won. He was stunned!

We played two more games that he won handily. I suspect I would never have been able to beat him again. I realized later how I had won that first game. He thought, as he said, that I had a strategy. I didn't! The Chaos Theory reigned! I was not restricted by the trodden paths.

This example illustrates why someone who is not confined to established protocols can occasionally jump past all the shrapnel of preconceived restrictions.

Lesson #8: To get more comfortable outside the box sometimes you have to take off your company tie and manly earring and slide into a pair of Paul Bond boots.

In a Nutshell

So much of success depends on the ability and willingness to make decisions. It makes sense to learn everything you can about a problem or project, consult with authorities, read the instructions, and study the history, doesn't it? Of course it does, but then you look at the stock market, talk to the broker's therapist, and listen to the screaming. And they all claim to know what they are doing!

I do not mean to diminish the usefulness of examining an issue thoroughly before making a decision, but most successful entrepreneurs did not achieve their pinnacle by betting on a sure thing. It was a great training ground for someone whose specialty was going to become poetry.

CHAPTER 2

It Is Illegal to Publish Poetry in the United States

The Western Writers of America is a distinguished group. They are the torchbearers for the likes of Zane Grey, Louie L'Amour, and Elmer Kelton. I have several friends and mentors among them. In June of 1983 they invited me to address their meeting. I was honored, even though most of the heroes in their books lived in the 1800s, and mine are getting bucked off or run over in modern times.

They put me on the mailing list for their quarterly journal. The editor was a good writer and invited me to submit a piece. I sent in a poem. He wrote back to explain that the Western Writers Association does not include cowboy poetry as part of western writing, nor do they print it in their journal. I sent him a little piece about how it was illegal to publish poetry in the United States. He laughed, but they didn't change their policy.

Many years later after Elko, Nevada, invented the cowboy poetry gathering model, I noticed the WWA began including it as an awards category.

Let me give you another example of the prevailing opinion of poetry in the last one hundred years that continues to this day.

In May 1986 I got invited to entertain at the Tejon Ranch at the south end of the San Joaquin Valley in California. They had Hereford cattle, thousands of acres, and the last California condor on Earth.

While at the ranch I met the publisher of the *Bakersfield Californian* (approximately 100,000 circulation). He wanted to run my weekly column in his newspaper. I was thrilled!

Lesson #9: It is always a blessing when manna falls from Heaven! But don't take it for granted and don't count on it again.

He reasoned that it would appeal to the large agricultural community in Kern County. He instructed his managing editor to start carrying the column. The editor resisted. I called and made the proper arrangements with him and answered his questions. But it took several weeks to get it up. When he finally did, I noticed he wasn't running all of them. I called.

The editor explained that their newspaper policy prohibited the publication of poetry. I pointed out that poetry constituted 25 percent of my columns! Each month included a poem. That's too bad, he said . . . I thought I heard him cackling.

I conceded he could do what he wanted because he was the editor, but would he please tell me why they don't print poetry.

"Most of it is bad," he explained.

"Well," I said, "you're an editor. You're supposed to be able to tell if it is good writing or bad. Just read the poems and decide." I thought my logic was crystal clear.

"I don't have to," he said. "We don't print poetry." His logic was crystal clear. *Catch-22*

I had the feeling that he was looking for a way to keep me out of his paper, but he still had to justify it to his boss, the publisher. "Tell me the real reason," I persisted.

"Off the record?" he said. "The publisher's wife writes poetry and if I printed yours, I'd have to print hers!" ***Checkmate***

I also suspect he resented the publisher telling him what to print. But, in truth, a poet could never have gotten into his office in the first place! Even with an agent or syndicator! In my case I couldn't have found a better introduction than the publisher . . . yet it wasn't enough.

Okay, I figured, maybe three times a month would be all right, but then he put me on the editorial page alternating weekly with Louis Rukeyser's column. He was leaving out my funny columns, which eliminated the majority of them. "You need to do more serious commentary on agri-business," the editor said. "Can you just write more columns with substance?"

I whined that the main reason my column was popular with the publisher was that it was funny. ***Brick Wall***

In retrospect it was a pretty smooth maneuver. He isolated me then locked me out. But he did it in such a way that he had something to tell the boss that made me look like the goat.

I conceded after a year and quit sending them the columns.

Lesson #10: Always remember it is the job of editors, program directors, producers, and publishers to keep you off the air and out of print. You are just more work for them, something new they have to deal with. Without an agent, manager, or cousin in the business, or a history of national misbehavior and disgrace, you are invisible to them. Don't take it personally. I repeat . . . Do Not Take It Personally.

Around that same time I was going on the Nashville television guest shows like Ralph Emery, Crook & Chase, and Nashville Now doing cowboy poetry. My self-published poetry book sales through 1986 were 49,205, and I did ninety-five speaking engagements across the country that year. I was a cowboy poet!

Hee Haw approached me to be on their show. Great! I'd fit right in, I thought. I could come to Nashville for a couple days, record twenty-six separate poems, and become a star! I remember figuring how many different shirts I should take.

"Oh," they said, "we want you to play a country hick veterinarian. That poetry won't work. People don't like poetry."

The evidence of my modest success as a poet, even including attracting the attention of *Hee Haw* producers, was not enough to overcome their ingrained ubiquitous aversion to poetry. It is just as strong today in most circles as it was then.

When I first started entertaining professionally, meaning I had lost my veterinary job and was interviewing for another, my business card said *Cowboy Humorist and Veterinary Consultant*. It did not include the word "poet."

I recall during that time period being in the lobby of a high school gym before the show began. A ranch wife came striding by with a scowling husband in her wake. She smiled as she passed. He glared at me.

I had seen it before; the wives weren't turned off that I was a poet, but the husbands were often attending under duress! Later after the show I was signing a book for that same lady. She had enjoyed the show. The rancher hung back, kinda givin' me the eagle eye.

"Well," I asked the man in a kindly way, "what did you think?"

"Shoot," he said, "I didn't even know it was a poem till you were halfway through it!"

Lesson #11: Sometimes it's okay to ride a Trojan horse into the game as long as you don't make a fool of the horse or the Spartans.

Shutterstock

In the United States poetry is held in low regard by most in the publishing and writing business. It is ironic that one of the highest compliments a reviewer can make is that something is "almost poetry."

By the turn of the nineteenth century Robert Service, Edgar Allan Poe, and Rudyard Kipling were being memorized and quoted by the American masses. In Australia, at the same time, Banjo Paterson and Henry Lawson were published regularly in the *Sydney Herald*. Even today schoolchildren revere them. Since the 1800s poets Alexander Pushkin in Russia and Jose Hernandez in Argentina have been and are still recognized by their common countrymen as national treasures.

So it was that at the last quarter of the twentieth century I chose to become a poet. It is common to evaluate someone's success by the amount of money they earn. Since you can count on one hand (a slight exaggeration) the number of people who make enough money as a poet to buy a used car, I chose to define success differently.

Being a poet is like being a golfer. You are sitting on the plane, and the person next to you asks if you golf. "You bet," you say. "I play a little."

"What do you do for a living?" she asks.

"I work for social services."

Or you ask another person, "Are you a poet?"

"Sure am! It's right here on my business card."

"What do you do for a living?" you ask.

"Oh, I work at the feed store," or "I'm an English teacher," or "I train horses."

To me credibility as a poet is not measured by how many books you sell, poetry is in the ear of the beholder. If they think what you write is poetry, then you are a poet. Maya Angelou writes poetry. She is also a college professor, a dancer, an administrator, and a best-selling author. Jimmy Carter writes poetry. He's an ex-president, but he does not depend on his poetry to make a living; he gets a pretty good pension!

When I heard Terry Gross's interview with Ted Kooser stating that "You'll never be able to make a living writing poems," I was not surprised. Although in his case maybe I should have been. He was at the time the reigning Poet Laureate and Pulitzer Prize winner in poetry. His poetry is in a league all its own. He deserved the recognition. It was a wonderful interview. But he was modest and explained that he had always had to have steady employment. He had been in the insurance business.

UNL Publications and Photography

Ted Kooser

Lesson #12: Caution to budding poets, entrepreneurs, and ex-presidents: Don't jump off the old train till the new train is running the same speed. In other words, don't give up your day job!

In a Nutshell

From the end of the Robert Service–Rudyard Kipling era circa 1920s until the rise of the Cowboy Poetry Gatherings in 1985, poetry was in the hands of what is loosely called academic poets.

Academic poetry is a treasure in its own right, but for whatever reason you would like to choose, it is not very popular. There are exceptions, of course—Robert Frost was one. I should recognize that several cowboy poets were active and read in the early 1900s by the western ranching community: Gail Gardner, Curly Fletcher, Bruce Kiskaddon, and Badger Clark, to name a few. Arguably, the most recognized was S. Omar Barker, whose work was appreciated on a larger scale.

But everything changed in 1985. The first Cowboy Poetry Gathering in Elko, Nevada, exploded upon the literary scene and changed the perception of poetry for a nation! Cowboy poets and their poetry were being presented on The Tonight Show, *in* Newsweek, *the* New York Times, People Magazine, USA Today, *the* Wall Street Journal, *the* Christian Science Monitor, *on the BBC, and NPR, and today the words "cowboy poet" still bring a positive image to most folks' minds.*

The preeminent poem of the century was written by Wallace McRae. The title of that poem is "Reincarnation."

Cowboy poetry is still riding high and has raised the level of awareness for all kinds of poetry as well as western music. But is it literature? The question is moot; it doesn't pass the "so what?" test.

It is obvious to me that, today, poetry is accepted less suspiciously by a wider circle, particularly among what could be loosely designated "the common man." Alas, due to its continued rejection by the large percentage of print media, it still can be said that "it is illegal to publish poetry in the United States."

Courtesy of Sue Roseoff

ʟᴏꜱᴛ ɪɴ ᴇʟᴋᴏ
by Sue Roseoff

CHAPTER 3

The Making of a
Self-Sustaining Poet

In my business the poet, me, is the product as much as the poetry books, CDs, and DVDs that we sell. My financial statement has three categories:

1. Speaking engagements.
2. Media, which include a weekly column, a weekly radio program, a weekly TV program on RFD-TV and U.S. Farm Report, plus producing radio and television commercials and doing voice-overs.
3. Product sales: books, audio books, CDs, and DVDs, and I also have a few cows.

Lesson #13: When it takes more than ten minutes to explain what you do for a living, you are self-unemployed!

When asked how I make a living, I reply that I do "agricultural banquets," or speaking invitations. Typical appearances include the

Governor's Agricultural Conference in Dover, Delaware; the Louisiana Radio Networks Farmer of the Year Award banquet in Baton Rouge, Louisiana; the Back Country Horseman's Fund Raiser in Omak, Washington; the Central Plains Dairy Expo in Sioux Falls, South Dakota; the Massachusetts Veterinary Association 125th Anniversary in Framingham, Massachusetts; the National Cowboy and Western Heritage Museum in Oklahoma City, Oklahoma; the Two Shot Goose Hunt in Lamar, Colorado; the National Association of Urologists, county fairs, rodeos, trail rides, FFA banquets, Student Chapter of the American Veterinary Medical Association (SCAVMA) conventions, and the occasional public radio fund-raiser.

That is a long way from the daily life of a hardworking large animal veterinarian with his hand up the back of a cow or in a horse's mouth! But how did I become a veterinarian in the first place? Like most of the life-altering changes in my life, it wasn't very well planned!

Lesson #14: Keep your shoulder to the wheel but don't take your eye off the road.

I started working at Bumper's Grocery in Mesilla Park, New Mexico, when I was fourteen for 60 cents an hour. I worked after school and weekdays from 3:30 to 6:15 p.m. and eight hours on Saturday. Christmas of 1958 I received a leather carving kit. I recall not being very pleased with the gift, but my records show that I sold my first custom handmade belt in September of 1959 for $2.79 to my childhood friend, Conrad Oman.

I worked for Bumper's Grocery until December of 1961. I quit the job to go out for the high school wrestling team. I had never gone out for a sport before; I was always working. By January 14, 1962, my leather record book showed I had carved ninety-two belts for a total of $227.17. So even when I wasn't working for wages I brought in some income by carving leather.

Shutterstock

Upon graduation from high school in 1962, I took a minimum-wage job working for a sheep parasite research facility at New Mexico State University in Las Cruces, the town where I lived. It was not a technical job; I was the sheep holder, as in, "Hold that sheep!" I cleaned pens, collected samples at the packing house, washed laboratory equipment, and was generally the sheepherder. I held that job full-time summers, part-time during college semesters, played rhythm guitar in a little band, and rode a few bulls in

the local and college rodeos through the three years until June 1965. Total belts carved to date: 136.

Toward the end of my sophomore year at New Mexico State majoring in animal science, I began to wonder what I would do with a bachelor's degree. I wanted to be in the cattle business, but I had no ranch to go home to and very little experience other than "holding sheep." I considered going to veterinary school. Not because I had any role models but based on the simple logic that when I graduated and went to some big livestock operation to apply for a job and they asked, "What can you do?" I could say, "I can fix your cow!"

I know it's not as warm and kindly as "I just love little animals," but everyone is different.

Unfortunately, there was only one thing standing between me and submitting my application to veterinary school: According to my advisor, I would have to take some required courses.

"Like what?" I asked.

"Well," he answered, "two four-hour semesters of organic chemistry . . ."

"I already took organic chemistry," I protested.

"This," he replied, "is the real organic chemistry!"

He then outlined how I would also need two four-hour semesters of physics and a five-hour calculus and trigonometry class.

All that before I could even apply.

"No sweat!" I said like a blindfolded man in front of a firing squad. "Take yer best shot!"

I enrolled in the first round of organic chemistry and physics, putting off the dreaded calculus and trigonometry. That fall I dove feetfirst into my new curriculum! They had drained the pool! By mid-semester I was going to the bottom like a set of car keys!

The organic chemistry looked vaguely familiar, but physics left me baffled. To this day I have never understood the significance of a steel ball rolling off a four-by-eight sheet of plywood!

The draft board was a real part of a young man's life in those days. They watched prospective draftees like hawks. I knew if I didn't get into vet school they would not look favorably on me changing my major again and staying around another year. To hedge my bets I went down to the Navy recruiter, who did a brisk business enlisting cowboys who had never seen the ocean.

The recruiter welcomed me. I explained that I was exploring my options in case I didn't get accepted to vet school. My plan was to join the Navy before I got drafted by the Army.

"Great!" he said. "What do you want to do?"

"I wanna fly them jets off the carrier!" I said with vigor.

"Super!" he said. "We're lookin' for boys like you."

I took the physical exam and the test for Officer's Candidate School. Passed them both.

"Are you ready?" he asked, grinning like a man standing above a shark tank.

"No! No," I objected. "I still have a chance for vet school!"

I finished that semester with a C in organic chemistry and a D in physics. I was thrilled!

Shutterstock

In January I lined up on another round of chemistry, another round of physics, and the five-hour calculus and trigonometry course. Let me tell you what that was like. Every weekday morning at 8:00, I walked into this huge auditorium filled with four hundred engineering students. Although *Star Wars* hadn't been invented yet, it was like boarding the Death Star. Everybody around me had a short haircut and was in ROTC.

I sat in the back row (where people like me sit) so I couldn't see the blackboard. The professor was a Nobel Prize winner from Pakistan, and I couldn't understand him anyway.

As if that weren't enough torture, the course included a two-hour math lab every Saturday morning. It was like getting your prostate examined every weekend!

By mid-semester I was losing the battle. I had sent my application to Colorado State University Veterinary School but was not optimistic. I decided I better check in with the Navy recruiter again to see if I was still eligible.

"Nope," he said. "You've expired."

I took the tests again. Again he tried to sign me up.

"It won't be long," I said. "Things aren't looking good. I've sent in my application, but if it's declined, I'm gonna quit school and come enlist."

Somewhere around April Fool's Day I received my letter from CSU. I carried it around all day, not wanting to open it in public. That evening back at home I opened it. It read: "You have been accepted to Veterinary School at Colorado State University . . . contingent . . . on passing the remaining courses."

Accepted! Unbelievable!

I had a month left to save myself. I redoubled my efforts . . . started going to class . . . and by the time I took the finals that spring, I knew more about organic chemistry, physics, and calculus and trigonometry than I would ever know again in my life.

They posted the grades on Saturday morning. I went around to see how I did. Chemistry . . . a C! Yeah! Physics . . . a D! *Allll right!* I went to the little building on the south side of the Horseshoe where my weekend math lab took place. I was standing in the hallway trying to see the grades that had been posted on the wall. The place was packed. Honor student–looking people with slide rules swinging at their hips and a pocket full of penholders were jostling to find themselves on the list.

I worked my way to the front and began reading: "Baca, Baker, Balderrama, Beltran, Black . . . F.

I had flunked the course.

I heard the strains of, "Anchors away, my boys, anchors away—"

"Wait," I said, "maybe there's a clerical error!"

I climbed in line to visit with the graduate student who had taught the math lab. I was behind this big tall man. When his turn came to talk to the instructor, he was complaining because he had received a B plus. She explained that he had gone into the finals with a 90 average but had only gotten an 89 on the finals. "You can do the numbers," she said.

He hummphed off, grumbling.

Suddenly I was standing in front of the person who held my future in her hands. I don't know if you can picture a math graduate student in the '60s. They weren't paid well and were overworked. She had worn the same pair of scruffy sandals all year. She didn't have time for a lot of personal grooming. I knew she had a child because you could see Gerber stains on her peasant blouse. She had tried to iron her hair flat in the Peter, Paul, and Mary style, but it didn't work. She mostly looked like she had her hair on crooked.

I did what any normal person on the brink of self-immolation would do—I dropped to my knees. I rapidly explained my situation:

All I had to do was pass. It was vet school! I was looking up at her, actually up her nostrils, but it was hard to concentrate with the peace symbol at eye level swinging in her cleavage.

She adjusted her John Denver glasses and looked at her clipboard.

"Mr. Black," she said, "you went into the finals with a 54 average."

"I know," I said, "I was comin' on strong!"

"But you flunked the final exam," she said.

"Ya know," I pleaded, "I don't know what to say. I was here every Saturday morning, right back there in the back, regular as an insulin shot. And I could come back here for the next ten years and never begin to grasp what in the world you are talking about! There is nothing more I can do."

A moment passed. The clock ticked. I was tied to a rocket, and she was holding the match.

"Mr. Black," she said straight-faced, without pity or disdain, "I will give you a D minus on one condition."

I said, "Anything." And I meant it! Whether it was doing her laundry all summer or chewing old buffalo hides to make her some new sandals . . . I was ready. She spoke, "A D minus, if you promise never to take calculus or trigonometry again!"

I kissed her stickery ankles, and she said, "Next."

That spring semester of my third year in college I made a 1.8 grade point average. I had taken a one-hour weight lifting course to bring up my grades!

Lesson #15: There are people who profoundly change your life. Sometimes they don't even know it.

I took a summer job on the San Agustin Plains of New Mexico and made a little money riding bulls. The fall of 1965 I moved to Ft. Collins, Colorado, to begin veterinary school.

It was apparent right away that holding a job while trying to go to vet school was impossible for most students, including me! I began setting up enterprises. Every Christmas and Easter break I would drive back to Las Cruces to spend time with Mother and the brothers. I would make the hour-long trip south to Ciudad Juarez, Mexico, and buy modestly priced silver buckle sets, boots, cheap blankets, and trinkets to resell. On the return trip to Colorado I would swing through Taos, New Mexico; and pick up a select few higher-dollar turquoise buckle sets and items.

The summer of my sophomore-junior year in vet school I was given a ticket for driving too fast in Texas, too slow in California, and for passing a policeman on a double yellow line in New Mexico; I achieved the traffic citation Grand Slam!

Back in Colorado I could offer customers hand-carved belts or purses, or custom requests. The going price for a carved belt was $5.

One trip I bought a pair of fancy Mexican boots. They were black, handmade, had an eagle on the front and dog-ears on the side. They cost me $18. I sold them that fall for $24, but the buyer said they were just a little tight. Unfortunately, he had already bought and worn them. I suggested the cowboy method of stretching them by stuffing them with dry pinto beans, then filling the boot up with water.

It stretched them so well it popped the seams, and he said it was years before he got all the beans out of the toe! He was not a repeat customer.

Over the years I had learned some barbering skills and began to cut hair. It was mostly for the veterinary students. "Quarter haircut for a dollar!" was my sales pitch. It eventually became a good sideline.

The veterinary clinic gave me a room upstairs where I put an old beauty parlor chair I had picked up at the thrift 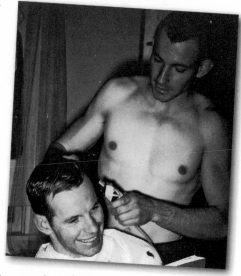 store. Truman Smith, a fellow student from New Mexico who also cut hair, became my partner.

I lived off campus, and one of my roommates was a musician. He and I teamed up with a veterinary classmate from Montana who was a good singer and could play lead guitar. We formed a band called "Los Mulas Musicales." By the time we were juniors we were playing regularly around the area.

I was able to rent a bass, bass amp, and microphone from a local music store for $5 a night. Our regular Saturday night gig was at the Hide-A-Way in Livermore, twenty miles north of Ft. Collins. We were paid $50 total per night. That covered the $5 for the rental, and left $15 for each musician. We played from 8:00 p.m. to 1:00 a.m.

In my junior year I inherited the laundry concession. The students had a regular flow of dirty, bloody, snotty, cow-pucky, cat-peepy, dog-poopy coveralls and smocks. As students we'd go through two or three garments a week. My classmates would toss their dirty clothing in a big box. The laundry man would pick it up and deliver them cleaned, folded, and sparkling. I would pay him for the whole batch.

Each garment had the student's name embroidered on it. I would sort them all, lay them out, and write down the names of the recipients, who would then pay me for the service. I, of course, made a modest profit for my labors.

One cold afternoon when I was a junior, I was in small animal surgery watching Dr. Smith spay a dog. Upon completion he popped off his latex gloves, pulled down his mask, and said, "Okay, meet me back here in fifteen minutes. I'm going to get a cup of coffee."

We students trudged back to the locker room and hung around just killing the fifteen minutes. I realized the doctor had gone for coffee, which would have been nice for us, too, but the nearest coffee was the student Sub two blocks away. We were in our smocks. There was no time to change clothes, go for coffee, then redress and make it back to surgery. A light went on in my brain!

On the way home from school I went by the pawn shop and bought a two-gallon coffeemaker previously used by Theodore Roosevelt at the Battle of the Little Bighorn. It consisted of two giant pots separated by a metal sieve screen. It all sat on top of a big hot plate burner.

Then I went by the A&P and picked up five pounds of the strongest, cheapest "floor sweepings" I could find. Next morning I arrived at the locker room at 6:30 a.m. I filled the bottom tank with water and put it on the hot plate. It took thirty minutes to heat up the water. I filled the screen with coffee, and with the dexterity of a juggler I managed to pour the gallon of hot water into the top container, set the empty bottom container back on the hot plate, set the screen full of coffee on top of the bottom container, and set the top container full of hot water on top of the screen and put the lid on.

It filtered down through and . . . Voila! There was fresh coffee in the locker room for the junior and senior classes! I kept the hot plate plugged in until noon, at which time I would repeat the process, adding some water, pouring it back through the used grounds. I would switch off the hot plate at 3:00 p.m., and when everybody left at 5:00 p.m., I would clean up the coffee mess and get ready for the next morning. I was the first person there every morning and the last to leave. *The world is run by those who show up.*

After a couple tries at asking folks to put a nickel in a jar for every cup, I eventually wound up charging those who wanted coffee by the month. That way I knew who was signed up and I could monitor the group around the coffee-pot to keep the others honest.

Shutterstock

By our senior year I was making $50 a week off my enterprises. I would post a bill every month on the bulletin board listing charges under each class member's name for coffee, laundry, haircuts, and custom services.

Each summer I had taken a job in a feedlot; the first in Roswell, New Mexico, then Thermal, California, and finally Ewa Beach, Hawaii. I rode pens, worked on the doctor crew, drove the molasses truck and front-end loader. I usually averaged $300 per month in wages working six days a week. Wednesday was usually my day off.

My final entrepreneurial coup in veterinary school was the publication of our own class annual, *Retained Memories 1969*. Normally, in the giant school-wide CSU annual, the only place veterinary students appeared was two pages between the engineering class and the wildlife majors. These two pages contained four group photos of the vet students, one for each class. If you looked with a magnifying glass, you could maybe pick someone you knew out standing on the bleachers. We looked like a chain gang reunion!

The first step toward self-publication of the annual was to get a professionally done formal head shot of each class member. I called a local photography studio and asked what he would charge to take my graduation photo. He told me.

I asked if he could give me a break if I could arrange for my entire class of sixty to come to him. We struck a bargain.

Next I borrowed some official stationery with the Veterinary School heading. I typed and posted a letter informing senior students that the official veterinary school graduation photos would be taken at the aforementioned studio, and I listed the dates. I restricted it to three days.

Lesson #17: I have learned that in most cases it works best to keep times tight, whether it's a special bargain on the web page, or a mailer buy two–get one free offer, or graduation photos. Buy now! Buy now! Buy now!

I posted the price each student would be required to pay that the photographer and I had agreed on, which covered his costs and supplied me a copy of each student photo at no charge. I can't remember whether I used the dean's office or a fictitious name as the signatory.

It worked like a charm! The annual turned out to be one of the class's more valued souvenirs. Despite my intentions, I didn't make a dime on it. It became a giant class project and every member of the class helped, so each got their annual at cost. Oh, well, I guess I owed them for contributing so much to financing my education!

When I graduated, I sold my half of the barber chair to my hair-cutting partner, passed on the laundry concession, and gave the coffee machine to some starving underclassman. By the time of my graduation in 1969, I had made 201 belts. They were now going for $6 to $8 plus the optional silver buckle.

In a Nutshell

You can see from my early history that I was always looking for a way to market my wares or my time. The pressure to achieve was stimulated by the critical fact that veterinary school was so hard most students were not able to hold a steady part-time job and still keep up with the class work.

But in spite of my penchant for entrepreneurism in veterinary school, I doggedly looked forward to the security of getting a regular job "workin' for wages."

A Poet Enters the Real World

A question frequently asked of me is, "Were you always funny?" In response I quote my eighth grade teacher, Mrs. Rath, who said to me, "But you come from such a nice family."

I've always been comfortable talking to crowds. I was the president of my senior class in high school and the FFA. At New Mexico State University (NMSU) I was a class representative to the student council and the president of the Block and Bridle, the animal science club.

High School Senior

I think I owe whatever popularity I had to the perception that I was funny. I was never prom king, quarterback, or Big Man on Campus; those honors were reserved for more mentally or physically talented boys. They were so good they didn't have to be funny!

During my incarceration in veterinary school at Colorado State, I played in a western dance band. I was the front man, I sang. And again it was not because I was the most able or the most talented.

PICKIN' IT OUT

In time I graduated from three years at NMSU and four more at Colorado State University (CSU) as a doctor of veterinary medicine. I had the wonderful opportunity to practice my trade in the Wild West amongst the cowboys, sheepherders, ranchers, farmers, prospectors, guides, hunters, rodeo hands, coyotes, and cattle.

My profession required extensive travel over several states, going to ranches, feedlots, dairies, sheep camps, horse barns, feed mills, and big country. When I went to work cows in the fall, the job might take several days. The ranches were often isolated. This was in the era of no satellite or wireless connections, no videos, no cell phones. I'm reminded of an ad in one of the local ranch papers that read:

> **Wanted: Cowboy. No TV. No phone. If you don't like dogs and can't tough it in the mountains don't apply. Alamo, Nevada.**

I would show up at the ranches to do the pregnancy checking, bull testing, help with the calf branding, or occasionally marking the sheep. It took the whole crew often working daylight till dark three or four days in a row. In the evening we'd eat in the cookhouse, then I'd break out my guitar. I fancied myself a songwriter in those days. Sometimes one of the cowboys had an instrument. We played music and told stories till bedtime, then it was off to the bunkhouse. As I recall, they were joyful occasions. Of course, they were starved for entertainment! In the sheep camp we played *damas*. I could never beat the Basque herders at the game.

In southwestern Idaho, where I lived, I participated regularly in several community festivities. Most of the "committee" assignments were guided by the Potato Salad Principle.

Lesson #19: A lady told me one time, "if you learn to make potato salad, the rest of your life it will be you who always brings the potato salad."

The committee would be planning a project and the discussion would go, "Okay, Joe, you're gonna be able to move all those panels, aren't you? You've still got your forklift? And the Echevarrias are going to man the concession booth, I'm assuming, and Margaret, you'll bring the potato salad . . . you always do . . ."

The equivalent of my "potato salad" was to act as master of ceremonies or pre-rodeo announcer, to play Bert Parks's role at rodeo queen contests, and to bring the sound system. For years I was the opening act for perspiring rodeo queen contestants, keynote speakers, eight-year-old barrel racers, and mutton busters. I always made myself available when work allowed.

I was certainly not polished professionally, but it was another case wherein the isolated sheepherders I entertained on the job probably had seen better in Barcelona, but I was the only one there!

Lesson #20: Remember, often it's not ability, it's reliability. The world is run by those who show up.

As Yogi Berra might have said, "When you come to a fork in the road, take it!"

The *Ventura County Star* in southern California had a love advice column wherein three local cowboys answered questions from letters. It was sort of a hairy-legged, tobacco-chewing version of Dear Abby. One of the letters to the column read: "*My wife has filed for divorce but she wants us to go to the marriage counselor so she can say she tried. What should I do? Signed, in the crosshairs.*"

"*Dear Crosshairs, CHANGE STATES!*"

The timing was perfect.

After eleven years of practice, I was offered a job with an animal health company. They needed a DVM who was competent to handle complaint calls and one who could comfortably speak to groups of producers and local veterinarians about disease entities in cattle, sheep, and horses. One of the tech vets, as they were called, had seen me speaking at a meeting somewhere and recommended me for the job.

I tendered my resignation to John Basabe and moved from Idaho to Denver to work for the animal health company. Very quickly I was swept up in the new job. The complaint calls were few, but each one carried a lot of responsibility.

The producer meetings were designed to educate customers, promote products, and improve public relations. The sales rep would line up a group of local veterinarians or livestock producers in his sales region and invite them to supper in a town. They were always fun, a night out for the farmer and his wife, and all compliments of the animal health company. Then I would rise and give them a thirty-minute presentation of pertinent animal health problems, and the sales rep would follow me with a talk on what products we had available to help these ailments.

I think my appeal can be laid directly at the hands of my stubbornosity. It was *de rigueur* at the time that presentations like mine be done with a slide show. They pointed out to me that 80 percent of people absorb knowledge visually. I asked, "What about the other 20 percent?"

"That's you," they said.

"How do you know?" I asked.

"You sing," they said, "and play music. You make funny noises." They explained I was an aural absorber.

Still, I refused to carry that case full of slides, even though I had wonderful slides of sick animals and pathological body parts from my own veterinary practice. But the slides were so heavy! It was like dragging an anvil around. And, hey, I was newly single, on the road, and travelin' light!

To compensate, I used humor to illustrate my points rather than slides. Thus, I was deemed more humorous than informative and, therefore, in demand! Within six months of my hiring on, the company was receiving requests from all over the country to have me come and speak at their livestock meeting.

It was an odd problem for the company. Normally they would have to compete with other companies and producer apathy to have the opportunity for a company rep or tech vet to be on their program.

One of the secretaries at the company headquarters in Kansas City took over the job of "booking" me. We worked together on scheduling, company approval, and transportation. With rare exceptions, the speaking jobs were done under the auspices of the company. In other words, they were paying me and it cost the producer group nothing.

Sometimes I would do a weekend job and get a small stipend from the group. According to my records in their employ, I worked nearly 80 percent of the weekends. In the two years I was with them I did 186 producers meetings.

It was also a freewheeling two years! I traveled the country, a new town every night, it seemed. I grew knowledgeable on the diversities that exist in different regions in the livestock business. From Providence to San Luis Obispo, from the turkey producers to the equine veterinarians, from the Southern Saskatchewan Sheep Growers/Stock Dog Trials to the Two Shot Goose Hunt in Lamar! It's the closest I ever came to being the bass man for a rock star!

I had begun writing the column and so was open to new experiences that might serve as inspiration. Although not all of them wound up being suitable material.

Lesson #21: If you are gonna be a writer, you have to have something to write about.

This lesson could actually be classed as a warning instead, depending on how deep you dip your cup in the river of life. I had a good doctor in Colorado during the first half of my life as an entertainer. I was lax about throwing my body into harm's way. After I told him one of my horrifying, daredevil experiences on the road, he asked, "You know how some people will take a drink to reduce their inhibitions?"

"Sure," I said.

"You need yours," he prescribed.

The summer I started my job with the animal health company, they moved me to Kansas City in June for a month to be "indoctrinated." I was single and in debt and maybe more open to adventure than usual. One Saturday I read in the paper about the blues singers in town and decided to go see one.

To put this story in historical perspective, Kansas City was just five years past a huge race riot that had divided and hurt the community. I had grown up a minority in New Mexico. My county, Doña Ana, was 65 percent Spanish-speaking. We did not experience the prejudice and animosity that seemed to foment in many metropolitan areas. I was not sensitive to the interracial suspicion and enmity that simmered in the melting pot of Kansas City. I saw that the blues singers were black but thought nothing of it.

I lit out from my rented town house in Lenexa and headed east. I found myself on Troost Avenue, which I later learned was the "Mason-Dixon" line of the city. One of my favorite health foods is barbecued ribs, and Kansas City is famous for their ribs!

I parked my blue company crew-cab long-bed three-quarter-ton pickup in front of a rib joint and walked right in.

After I had ordered, I asked the proprietor how I could find Thirty-Ninth and Jackson. He gave me a sideways glance and asked why I wanted to know. He was a black man. I explained what I had read in the papers about the blues singers and that one was playing at Walter's Crescendo Lounge. The address was Thirty-Ninth and Jackson.

He told me in a fatherly way that I should not go. It was not a good part of town. He recommended a couple other places, but they were urban disco bars. I thanked him for his advice but figgered I could find my own way and departed.

As I climbed up behind the steering wheel, the proprietor came outside, came around the front of my truck, and put a piece of paper in my hand. It had a phone number on it.

"What's this?" I asked.

"It's my phone number. Call me when you get in trouble."

In retrospect one would think I should have been concerned, but I can say honestly that I was oblivious to his subtlety. It never occurred to me that I would not be welcome.

Half an hour later I pulled into a shady parking lot in front of a cinder-block building with beer signs in the windows. It was still daylight. I walked in and ordered a scotch and soda.

"You mean a cream soda?" asked the lady bartender.

The conversation went downhill from there. I was approached by an older gentleman. I reached to shake his hand, but he didn't reciprocate. He suggested under his breath that I might be more comfortable someplace else.

I walked into the adjoining dance hall and took a seat at an eight-foot banquet table in front of the stage. Over the next thirty minutes the place filled up with folks. They were dressed to the nines! I remember how colorful they were. They seated themselves at the booths and tables surrounding the dance floor yet I remained alone at my table. Then the music began!

It was one giant happy room! People dancing and partying. I asked several girls to dance with me, but they refused. At the end of the first set, the lead singin' guitar man jumped down off the stage, came right up to me, leaned into my face, and asked me what the heck I was doin' there. He was not friendly.

I said, "I heard this was the best blues music in all Kansas City and I come to find out."

He furrowed his brow, then said, "You did?"

"Yup," said I.

"Really?" he said, "Where did it say that?"

"In the paper."

"No kiddin'."

"Shornuf." I said.

He kinda stood back and tried to keep from smilin'. "Well? Whatta ya think?"

I said, "It's dang sure the best I ever heard!"

He did a little shoulder shrug and said, "How 'bout dat!" He reached out and shook my hand, put his other on my shoulder, and asked if I was bein' treated okay.

"Well," said I, "I could use another cream soda . . . and there won't nobody here dance with me."

"Beulah!" he yelled to the bartender. "Take care of my man here . . . don't let his glass go dry!"

Next thing I know there are three ladies sitting at the table with me, and we danced the night away!

Shutterstock

After two years the inevitable merger of two giant pharmaceutical companies came between me and a steady job. I have often thought that every two years the owners of the five or six major drug companies in the world get together in Zurich and play cards for the companies.

Shutterstock

The problem for the workforce is, when the companies combine there are people with overlapping talents or regions, and someone's gotta go! I was a casualty of the merger. Their logic was correct; I was the new man with the least seniority, and even though I was popular . . . well, let me quote a really good veterinarian and my supervisor at the company, who said of me, "He is a good veterinarian in many respects, but he is a management nightmare!"

At the time I was laid off, dismissed, fired, booted out, got the pink slip, or whatever is politically correct, there were still several producer meeting commitments that the company had obligated me to. "What should I do?" I asked. "Call and cancel?" They surmised that would be bad public relations to cancel, so they offered to pay me a fee for each of the prebooked jobs, approximately twenty of them. Ideal for me, except I was out of a job, and ideal for them since they got me off the company insurance! They called me a consultant, which is what professional people call themselves when they are between jobs.

THE CONSULTANT

Bein' in between jobs ain't no picnic.
In fact it's downright insultant.
So I printed some cards, put signs in the yard,
and bingo, became a consultant!

I solicited quality rest stops
in search of the right clientele.
Passed out ballpoint pens to all of my friends,
got an answer machine from Ma Bell.

At last an ol'-timer sought my advice.
He brought in his last balance sheet.
I saw with a smile that his management style
was outdated and obsolete.

So I set out to solve all his problems,
I spoke like a preacher possessed!
He sat there amazed, his eyes sorta glazed,
I could see he was truly impressed!

He said not a word as I rambled on.
For effect I went over it twice.
When time had expired, he politely inquired,
"How much for this expert advice?"

I said "Fifty bucks!" I thought it was fair.
From his looks I thought I could fake it.
But he nodded his head and finally said,
"Well, son, I don't think I'll take it!"

I had hired a woman to be my secretary several months before my dismissal, unaware of the impending merger. At the time I decided that I might need some help with the column. I had also published my first book by then. In addition I had some personal projects I thought she could help me with.

She worked two hours a day, three days a week, and could bring her baby to work. The workplace was the front room of my two-room apartment. The ad I put in the Denver paper that brought her to me was:

> **Struggling but busy songwriter needs help pushing songs. Happily married housewife preferred.**

She organized my "notebook full of livin' room hits" and started exploring the music business in Nashville. Then she took over typing, sending out, and billing my weekly column. When the company let me go, she began the process of booking me for speaking jobs. To my ultimate good fortune, even after I left the company, people continued to call with speaking requests. But things had changed . . . suddenly my services weren't free! Many callers weren't prepared to pay; they wanted the freebie that the animal health company had offered. But others discussed the price and negotiated with my secretary and hired me.

Confession #1: The biggest factor that influenced my continuing to avoid getting a job then was that I did not have to solicit the speaking engagements. It was all word of mouth.

I have to admit that I did not pretend it was a real job . . . speaking, that is. I was just doing it but keeping my veterinary licenses current. I did several employment interviews with livestock operations along the way, but I never managed to sign up. I also had occasion to make a few veterinary "consulting" calls during this time.

I married for the second time, managed to get out of debt, but still made the effort to keep up the continuing education required to practice veterinary medicine. There was another factor working in my psyche that kept me reluctant to let my veterinary career slip away.

Lesson #23: Giving up a regular paycheck to chase a cloud is scary to a person who's worked for wages all his life. Security is a wonderful, addictive lure. It eliminates so many worries.

WORKIN' FOR WAGES

I've worked for wages all my life, watchin' other people's stock
And the outfits I hired on to didn't make you punch a clock

Let you work until you finished! Like the feedlots in the fall,
When they roll them calves in on ya, they'd jis' walk the fence
and bawl.

We'd check the pens and pull the sick and push and treat and ride
Then process new arrivals that kept comin' like the tide.

And I've calved a lot of heifers though it's miserable sometime,
It's somethin' that I'm good at and it's like she's sorta mine.

She knows I ain't the owner but we're not into protocol.
She's a cow and I'm a cowboy and I guess that says it all . . .

Got no truck with politicians who whine and criticize
'Bout corporate agribusiness, I guess they don't realize

Somebody's gotta own 'em that can pay the entry fee!
Why, who they think puts up the dough to hire ol' boys like me?

Oh, I bought a couple heifers once maybe fifteen years ago.
I held 'em through a calving then I had to let them go

'Cause all I did was worry 'bout how to pay the bills.
Took the fun outta cow punchin', I don't need them kinda thrills.

Though I wouldn't mind a-ownin' me a little hideaway
So when some outfit laid me off I'd have a place to stay.

But I figger I'm jis' lucky to be satisfied at heart
That I'm doin' what I'm good at and I'm playin' a small part

In a world that's complicated where the bosses fight it out
With computers and consultants and their counterparts with clout.

They're so busy bein' bosses, they've no time to spare somehow,
So they have to hire someone like me to go out and punch their cow.

I grew up working. As a boy, a teenager, a college student, I worked. Worked for wages. My thirteen years of veterinary practice, I worked. I enjoyed it and drew great satisfaction in doing it.

I was very comfortable working long days, six or seven days a week, missed vacations, always on the job. They gave me a paycheck. That was my medal of success, my ten-year pin, my pat on the back, my daily confidence builder . . . that paycheck. My hobby was songwriting.

Not even in my wildest dreams could I have imagined saying to my wife, "I'm going to quit work and write songs. It's what I have to do to find my inner self. We can move to Nashville. Won't it be grand!" Of course not!

Any woman in her right mind whose husband was a professional man with a good paycheck, a nice car, horse trailer, and a home on the edge of town would slap him upside the head!

"What are you talking about, you moron?"

"Movin' to Nashville, being a glamorous songwriter . . ." I would say.

"Who's gonna make the car payments?"

"We'll ride the bus."

"Who's gonna feed the dog?"

"You can take him with ya!"

"Who do you think is gonna support us while you're going through this adolescent pipe dream?"

"Well, you did go to college . . ."

I can only say that I doubt I would have been able to voluntarily become an entertainer, to make that choice. It just wasn't in me. I was a good company man.

Confession #2: My replacement at the livestock company delivered me to the airport in my old company vet truck. He dropped me off at the curb. "Do you have everything?" he asked.

I looked down at my hangin' bag and guitar. I had sent my piano and my deer head to Denver with a hitchhiker. I fumbled a minute in my pockets. "Wait a minute," I said worriedly. "My keys . . . I can't find my keys." And then I realized I didn't have any keys. I had no car, no house, no bus station locker downtown, I was down to no keys.

I was thirty-five years old and starting over.

Had that few years of my life been different, I would most likely be a large animal veterinarian today, working for some big livestock operation with company insurance and a retirement plan. I'd probably still be funny, making up poems and telling stories to the cowboys, but dedicatedly working for wages. But sometimes your life gets taken out of your hands. The earthquake of divorce changed everything.

When people ask how I got to be an entertainer, I guiltily feel the need to explain, "I'm not doing it on purpose!"

I was divorced, lost everything, moved to another state, took a job that lasted two short years, then, at the peak of my bad luck, I was backed into the cauldron that created the businessman I have become. The entertainment business took over my life at a time when I had neither the willpower nor the incentive to resist it. I had no urge to settle back down and lead a normal life. When success came, I rode it all the way. One other essential ingredient: When I got married again, I married a woman who never once questioned how I make a living.

Lesson #24: No matter how good an agent, publicist, or fan base you have, make sure there is someone in your life who cares about the person inside the clown suit.

In a Nutshell

Becoming a financially successful poet, in my case, required going through "The Ordeal of Fire." It took four years. It was a tumultuous, heartrending, head-banging, bad-buckin', blindfolded, all-night, screw-loose, jet-propelled bronc ride that took me right to the edge and brought me back.

I dedicated this poem to a friend of mine who fell while sitting on a mule's neck backward and broke his back.

LIVIN' ON THE EDGE

There but for a whim of fate go you and you and I.
Any man who chases lightning or thinks that he can fly.
Are we stupid? Are we crazy? Are we rebels without cause?
No, the reason is much simpler. We bet the pot because
The drummer who keeps time for us stays just beyond the ledge
And one only hears his cadence when one's living on the edge.

Suffice it to say, most of the lessons I was taught during this stage of my life had to do with learning them the hard way. Going beyond the point of reason, stepping over the line, driving in life's fast lane with no seat belt.

I would suggest that there are much more sensible pathways to becoming a good businessman or a decent person. I am thankful that I survived myself. I see stories of overindulgent celebrities or politicians, poets, and CEOs who have fallen into ruin because they couldn't take their own lives back.

Lesson #25: If you ever have the opportunity to keep from making a fool of yourself . . . take it.

SECTION TWO

WHAT I LEARNED:

*To depend on my marketing ability
to survive,*

To think outside the box,

*And to appreciate the importance
of integrity.*

CHAPTER 5

Starting in the Book Business

I receive regular inquiries that begin, "I write poetry and my friends say I should write a book. How do I do it?"

My short response is:

Lesson #26: "Publishing a book is easy. All it takes is money!"

By the fall of 1980, while I was still practicing veterinary medicine, I had amassed a small collection of self-penned poems and a few stories (twenty-three, after culling). Several had become regulars that I used at the occasional master of ceremony or public speaking engagement, or trip to the ranch to check cows. Like many people who write poetry, I was being requested to do specific poems or for copies thereof.

That same year I had begun writing a weekly column for the *Record Stockman*, a livestock paper published in Denver. I did not

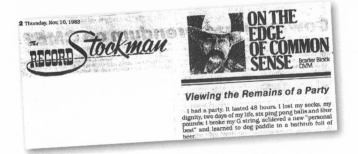

2 Thursday, Nov. 10, 1983

THE RECORD Stockman

ON THE EDGE OF COMMON SENSE   Baxter Black DVM.

Viewing the Remains of a Party

I had a party. It lasted 48 hours. I lost my socks, my dignity, two days of my life, six ping pong balls and four pounds. I broke my G string, achieved a new "personal best" and learned to dog paddle in a bathtub full of beer.

have much money and was deep in debt. I was single, living in a two-room apartment, driving a company car, paying alimony and ex-house payments, and traveling extensively as a consulting veterinarian for a large maker of animal health products.

I asked Harry Green, owner and publisher of the *Record Stockman*, about publishing a book of my poems. Harry had published a few books over the years in addition to his livestock paper. He agreed and would pay the cost to publish the books, oversee the process, and inventory the product. He sold them through his paper and paid me a royalty. I could buy them at publisher price to resell.

Lesson #27: One of life's business dictums: Somebody has to put up the money or nothing happens.

I enlisted the aid of a cowboy cartoonist and friend, Don Gill, to illustrate this first book. I put together the manuscript, and Harry set the type and had it printed. *The Cowboy and His Dog* was a seventy-six page softcover that measured 9 x 12 and was stapled with a color cover. It retailed for $7.95. The first printing was 1,000 books. I paid Donny a commission on books sold.

I began taking my book "on the road" with me. Harry advertised it in his paper. I started soliciting wholesalers like feed stores, saddle shops, co-ops, bookstores, and the Idaho Cattlewomen's Association. When the National Western Stock Show came around in January of 1981, I sat in the *Record Stockman's* booth for two weeks signing and autographing.

Many stores took my books on commission (they only paid me if they sold them). My accounting methods were pretty crude. I was drawing a paycheck from the company I was working for, so I could keep up with my debts. I always reported my sales receipts as accurately as I could. When you have a business that deals in cash, e.g., books sold on the road, it is easy to get in the habit of underreporting. I've never been tempted. There has almost always been a second layer of worker bees that benefits from the sale. In the beginning it was the artists who drew for me. Unreported book sales meant shortchanging them. The same went for employees who received a bonus based on sales.

Lesson #28: Honesty is the best policy—Life is less stressful if you aren't having to look over your shoulder at the people who are sorting through your droppings.

By 1982 I had enough material for a second poetry collection, *A Rider, Roper, and Heck'uva Windmill Man! Record Stockman* published that as well.

During the two-year period from July 1980 to September 1982, I remained in the employ of the animal health company and averaged approximately eighty-five to ninety speaking appearances a year on their behalf discussing animal health problems with producers and veterinarians. Although the content was seriously scientific, I illustrated my points with humorous poems. I had my books available afterward.

The end of 1982 showed 10,658 total book sales to date, with *Record Stockman* selling approximately 25 percent of inventory.

My veterinary job ended. The company changed hands and let me go. The company generously put me on as a "consultant" for another year to fulfill the speaking obligations they had made for me. Each new speaking request was now referred directly to me from the company. My secretary and I began booking the jobs ourselves.

In the fall of 1983, with *Record Stockman*'s help, I published a one-time run of 10,000 copies of a book called *On the Edge of Common Sense, The Best So Far*. It was a collection of non-poem columns I had written that were not included in the first two poetry books.

To celebrate the event I threw a party. I twisted the *Record Stockman* publisher's arm to help with the hotel bill, and I paid for the rest: food, refreshments, and transportation. I had asked several of the great cowboy cartoonists of the time—Ace Reid,

Colorado Carhartt

Jerry Palen, Lex Graham, Herb Mignery, Dick Spencer, Don Gill, and Bob Black—to illustrate four each of the stories included in *The Best So Far*. For the party I invited each of the cartoonists and their wives to spend the weekend in Denver to introduce the book to the press, and generally to get acquainted! The press was alerted, and I also asked several of my cowboy character friends to come and liven it up. My excuse for the bash was to get a group picture for the cover of the book.

You can see my thinking. I had great subjects who made the trip inside the book worth flipping through.

To take the cover photograph I hired the renowned western photographer Jay Dusard.

The party began. We cordoned off a wing of the Holiday Inn at the junction of I-25 and I-70. Several of us were musicians, everybody could tell jokes, we danced and partied, and, the icing on the cake . . . I had gotten married two weeks before! There amidst the revelry, I introduced the bride to my lunatic circle of friends. Some would have questioned the wisdom of throwing Cindy Lou into the whirlpool of my life with so little warning . . . but I have never overestimated her ability to tolerate the questionable behavior of my colleagues and to this day marvel at her inner strength.

Saturday morning Jay, the photographer, took us all out to a railhead on the grounds of the National Western Stock Show in Denver. He stood us in front and hanging off of a Union Pacific locomotive.

He distributed us in his lens. Jay's camera was a big box with a cloth hood just like those early photographers used in the Wild West after a hanging. He took his first exposure.

"Palen," said Jay, "you moved."

We lined up again. He exposed the glass. "Palen," he said again, "you moved."

He lined us up a third time and took the picture. "Okay," he said and turned to go.

I jumped down from the train. "Wait a minute, boys," I said to the cartoonists. "Let me make sure . . . Jay," I said, walking along beside him. He was carrying the big box camera and tripod, "Are you sure you got a good picture? I mean, Palen moved in the first two, and then you only took one. Don't you need a backup? I've got a Kodak here in my pocket. We could, wait a minute, Jay, I'm payin' you a thousand dollars, it's cost me a bundle to fly everyone in here, not to mention the two-day party, the hotel, shouldn't you—"

"I got the shot," said Dusard, never breaking stride.

"But, just in case—" I pleaded.

"I've got it," he said.

"Well . . ." I stammered. "Wait a minute, boys, line up there in front of the train . . ." but by then they were climbing in the vehicles and headed back to the hotel.

"I—"

Lesson #30: When Superman says he's got the cards, don't bet against him.

Suffice it to say the shot was good.

The book party stimulated a column. I enclose it here in its original form:

THE BOOK PARTY

I had a party. It lasted forty-eight hours. I lost my socks, my dignity, two days of my life, six Ping-Pong balls, and four pounds. I broke my G string, achieved a new "personal best," and learned to dog paddle in a bathtub full of beer!

The occasion for this all-out, climb the walls, cowboy shindig was in celebration of my new book. The party honored the world's best cowboy cartoonists who contributed cartoons for the book. We gathered under one roof some of the most unique individuals in the world of Western philosophy and art. Every one of them is a crossbred maverick of the finest kind.

Jerry Palen from Cheyenne showed up and spent Friday night tryin' to sell everybody a Shetland pony, sight unseen. The price went up Saturday after a phone call from his vet; it looked like the pony was gonna live!

In certain circles I am considered a pretty fair guitar picker (places like the 5th Amendment Bar after 11:00 p.m.). But I was relegated to playin' second fiddle to my brothers, Steve and Bob, Jim Schafer and my new wife.

Under the right circumstances I can be coerced into singin' a few ditties (as Champ Gross would say, "He'll sing to

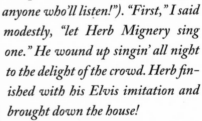

anyone who'll listen!"). "First," I said modestly, "let Herb Mignery sing one." He wound up singin' all night to the delight of the crowd. Herb finished with his Elvis imitation and brought down the house!

"Let ol' Bax sing one," he said. I did and everybody went to the bathroom.

I thought I could hold my own in storytellin'. But then Dick Spencer started tellin' about adobe submarines and his Indian relative, Running Bare. Pretty soon Ace Reid was spinning yarns about Lady Bird, Slim Pickens, Hondo Crouch and his old daddy, who claimed to be the best cattle thief in Texas.

Todd, Tink, and Andy each had more wild cow tales to fill in the empty spaces. All in all it was windier than a sack full of whistlin' lips.

I tried to be a good host and keep up, but two Idaho renegades, Don Gill and Gary Penny, were already walkin' on the window ledges and abusing the potted plants!

They came from all over. Don from Idaho, Radonna from Texas, Jack from Greeley, Champ from Wyoming, Mike from Longmont and my mother from New Mexico.

Bein' among these kinds of people was a blue ribbon treat. We did our best to make our own cowboy cartoonists feel special. But it's hard 'cause they're all just plain common decent folks like most of us and won't let you treat 'em different. Besides, I had to pay for the carpet in Don Gill's hotel room, Dick Spencer's check bounced, Sheri Mignery has a warrant out for my arrest, my brother Bob is changing his name, Jay Dusard is sending me his chiropractor's bill, the pony I bought from Jerry Palen didn't make it, and the ring Ace Reid sold me is turnin' my finger green!

Lesson #31: You will notice, on this grand occasion to help market my new book, I surrounded myself with a stunning array of talented, larger-than-life characters. Nothing attracts the crowd's attention like standing next to a person on fire.

One other incident happened that weekend that is worthy of note. The date of publication, the advertising, the press release, and the party were all planned around the release date of October 1, two weeks after the party. That would allow time for the cover to be printed and the book finished in time for the Christmas market.

The day before the party, Thursday, September 15, there was a fire in the publisher's warehouse and virtually all 10,000 copies of the printed books awaiting covers burned!

My secretary and right-hand person, Sheryl, had the forethought to take a box or two of the books without covers to the party to have them autographed by all the cartoonists and the photographer. They were the only ones not destroyed. The invitees and the cartoonists were each given copies. I would guess those copies are probably the rarest of all the books I have written.

To the credit of *Record Stockman* and the printers, they set up the presses and went after it. We had 10,000 copies of the book with its new cover in our hands in less than three weeks. Thanks to Mido Printing in Denver, Colorado!

The Best So Far sold over 5,000 copies that fall of '83 and was sold out by 1985. It was never reprinted.

During the approximately four years that I think of as "between wives," I had insomnia. I usually stayed up late writing songs and columns and poetry. Since I was not able to fill my insomniac hours with sleep, I began writing a novel based on the simple, stupefying logic that, if I was up anyway, I might as well do something productive. It took several months to write. I can't even tell you what it was about. I think I burned it.

Lesson #32: Don't bore your customers with mediocre material just because you wasted several months or years working on it. If you think it's good, remember you can always get a second opinon!

I began writing a second novel in 1981. It was a travelogue about two bull riders trying to make the National Finals Rodeo. I would go to bed in the apartment and write what I had thought up the night before. Then I would lie there thinking up the chapter I would write the next evening.

Years later, when the book was published and I was on a book tour, I would quote John Milton, famous English poet, when I was describing my insomnia. He said, "What hath night to do with sleep?" I told the crowd his quotation had become my mantra. It worked well until one night a fellow stood up in the back of the crowd and pointed out that, of course John Milton would say that . . . he was blind!

In those days I can remember listening to a ninety-minute sleep-inducing cassette that a psychologist had given me. I'd let it play out, reverse itself and play the other side, then click off. I'd turn it over and start again!

By Christmas of 1983 I had remarried and finished the rodeo novel. It was called *Hey Cowboy, Wanna Get Lucky?*

Pleased with myself, I made five copies of the four-hundred-page manuscript and mailed one each to the authors I thought would most appreciate my humor: John Nichols of *Milagro*

Beanfield fame; Dan Jenkins, who wrote *Baja Oklahoma*; Tom Robbins, author of *Still Life with Woodpecker*; Thomas McGuane of *Nobody's Angel*; and Hunter S. Thompson, *Fear and Loathing in Las Vegas*.

I did not know at the time the disposition of unsolicited manuscripts by the publishing world . . . **THE TRASH CAN.**

In my ignorance I waited expectantly. Then out of the clear blue I received a letter from Tom Robbins! He quoted me back to myself and finished by saying, "You need an agent, take mine!"

Lesson #33: Even when you do everything wrong, the occasional arrow-in-the-sky slips through the shrapnel and hits a target.

Tom's agent ran my manuscript up and down Madison Avenue. Every publisher said it needed to be rewritten and rejected it. Eventually the manuscript was retired to an upper shelf in my bedroom closet.

Subsequently, every other year I would publish a softcover book. Then octo-annually I would package the soft covers together in a hardback collection. Off years I would do cassettes, CDs, videos, then DVDs. The content consisted of selected poems and stories that had originally appeared in my column. The object was to have a new product every fall.

Out of the clear blue in 1992 I received a call from Crown Publishing, a division of Random House, offering to publish my poetry books! It was a dream call, one I never had considered happening, especially after my experience years before with the novel.

By December 31 of that year, my actual book sales (not books in print, a category New York publishers use as opposed to "books sold") were 210,329 poetry books including two two-hundred-page, 8 x 12, illustrated, hardback collections, retailing at $24.95.

As I listened to the publisher rep explain the rudimentary rules of how "Madison Avenue" worked, I felt less and less comfortable. My reservations had nothing to do with royalties, money, or editing; it had to do with ownership. If they published my poetry books, they would own them, with all the rights. Could I use the poems in my live programs? Could I make audio or video? Would I have to get their permission every time?

I made a decision during that first phone call before I hung up, which can be attributed only to a "gut feeling." I declined their offer. She tried to talk me out of it for my "own good." The advance in five figures, the royalties, the follow-up books. All with no financial investment from me, the author. I realize today that it probably was a very rare occurrence in her life, having an "unpublished" (which is synonymous with "self-published" in her world) author turn down Random House.

It is possible that over the next ten or so years I could have made millions more dollars and sold twice as many books had I accepted their offer. They have that power. And I wound up writing several more books and continue to, most of which I imagine they would have published.

I cannot say now whether the decision was bad or good. I only know that I have never regretted retaining the ownership of my poetry. In trying to explain what some would call a mule-headed cowboy mentality, I will call Leon Uris to my defense. In his book, *Mitla Pass*, his hero struggles in poverty for several years to write his first novel. Finally it is published and well received. He becomes rich and famous. Then Hollywood lures him to write screenplays and pays him exorbitant amounts of money. He cannot refuse, yet he is unsatisfied. He yearns to start his next novel, but he is too busy writing screenplays. He makes the distinction of "writing to have" and "writing to be."

I, too, make that distinction. The stories I write, the commercials, the novels are "writing to have." My poetry is "writing to be." I somehow knew that I did not want to give anyone that much control of what I am.

So, after I offered the Crown Publishing rep a gracious declination she asked, "Do you have anything else?"

I told her I had this old rodeo novel in my closet. At her request I mailed her the manuscript. She called back and said they would publish it if I rewrote it. I said, "Tell me how!"

I dusted off my agent and sent her into the fray.

In a Nutshell

Moving from the wilds of the Idaho backcountry with no keys to my name, to a point twelve years later being offered a contract from Random House, was a frenetic, unconventional passage. The book publishing part of my business sounds like a string of lucky breaks for someone who didn't really know what he was doing.

It is true that I didn't know exactly what I was working toward, but I never quit working. I wore away at the rocks in the stream as they constantly changed the course of my journey. Remember, I thought I was a songwriter!

You may read back through this chapter in search of guidance on how to self-publish your own books or CDs. First you need something that people will value and be willing to buy. Then you begin shooting arrows in the sky. However,

---

Lesson #34: Two pounds of persistence is worth ten pounds of talent.

You take advantage of every opportunity, then go back to those who said "no" last year, and try them again. Times change, editors, publishers, programmers, and purchasing agents change, and what you're offering changes.

Always be looking outside the box. There's nothing wrong with wearing a comfortable groove in your marketing methods, but if you dig yourself a rut, your potential customers can't see you anymore. Keep your hand in the air.

CHAPTER 6
Me and NPR

When my wife and I got married, she did not have a television, nor did I. We discussed it and didn't get one. It wasn't an issue with either of us. We were radio people living in the big Denver radio market. Local talk shows and country music were our fare, but for "national news" we became public radio listeners.

Morning Edition had begun in 1980. By the mid-'80s they were growing, but most of their focus was New York City and Washington D.C. Their funding did not allow them in-depth coverage of much else.

In 1988 Yellowstone National Park caught on fire. It raged, and smoke filled the western skies. In Colorado we could smell it in the air. Big range fires and grass fires spread across the western prairie. In the ensuing drought hundreds of thousands of acres were burned. It was a big part of our lives. NPR barely mentioned it. I realize now they had neither the time nor the money to give it coverage, or they probably would have.

Local public radio stations across the West were also growing, getting on their feet, and signing up with NPR. They gave our western natural disasters local coverage, but it never made the national radar.

By then I had been writing a weekly column for eight years and airing a weekly radio commentary on commercial radio networks in agricultural communities for two years. I had gone from recording them in my bathroom (seeking better acoustics) to building a house with a small studio complete with a reel-to-reel recorder! I became acquainted with knowledgeable electronics people. Thus I was capable of recording a high-quality tape.

I got the idea that NPR should be giving our burning West a little coverage. As I recall, the local NPR stations may have run some of my pieces, but it didn't give me any real credibility with the national network. I had written a long poem (five to six minutes) that summer called "Range Fire." I decided to send it and a couple others to NPR.

I should note that National Public Radio at the time was a "cozy-er, backyard friendly, neighborly" kind of network. Some would say "less professional," compared to the other national radio networks. It was one of the few networks, radio or television, where poetry did not seem out of place. Where the likes of Mark Twain or Will Rogers would have been welcome.

Today, NPR has progressed to the best national news provider, bar none, on radio and is respected worldwide. However, it is highly unlikely that my poetry would have the same appeal to their producers today as it did then.

But now is now, and then was then, and I was in the right place at the right time. Mind you, when I decided to send "Range Fire" to NPR, once again ignorance carried the day! Just like John Basabe's example, I was not hindered by knowing too much. I'm sure there must have been a protocol for submitting something to NPR. In my case, I didn't know a single person back there. I had no intro, no instructions, no agent, no union, just the hope that it would be received and listened to.

Keep in mind what had to occur for my piece to be aired. First, an unsolicited envelope, obviously containing a small reel-to-reel tape, had to be accepted by **Person #1**, whoever picked up the mail. I had much experience over the years sending unsolicited songs on cassette to music publishers. I should have known better; the disposition of unsolicited material to Nashville music publishers is well known . . . **THE TRASH CAN!** But still I sent my poem to NPR.

Person #1 who picked up the mail, probably a secretarial-type person, had to pass it on or put it in the trash. It was addressed simply to National Public Radio, 635 Massachusetts Ave. NW, Washington DC 20001.

Then, **Person #1** gave it to **Person #2** (probably an intern), in charge of the letter opener. **Person #2** could have opened it, read the accompanying letter addressed to Dear Sir, then passed it on up the line to **Person #3**, someone with credibility. Or **Person #2**, in charge of the letter opener, at any stage of the process could just as easily have tossed it in the trash!

Third, **Person #3**, someone with credibility, might not have had time to listen, might have listened but didn't like it, might have used it to wedge a table leg, might have set it on a shelf somewhere, just tossed it, or, as I'm guessing in my case, that particular morning, listened to it.

Fourth, **Person #3** would need to refer it up to **Person #4**, someone with the authority to decide, probably the producer, who then had to listen and give it a thumbs up or thumbs down.

You will read my axiom often in this book that . . . "It is the publisher's, editor's, and producer's job to keep you off the air and out of print." It is not to be taken personally. *Let me repeat,* it is not to be taken personally. Think of yourself as flotsam on the stream in which they are dangling their feet. Their hands are busy, and their minds are occupied elsewhere. Something new is like a buzzing fly.

Included in the factors of the producer's or editor's decision (often, the least of which is will the audience like it) are larger considerations, like "Who is this person? Do we really want to get involved? We already have too many commentators. Can we afford another one? Why do we have to keep changing? Does he fit our program agenda? Will he be competition? Is he manageable? It's a pain in the butt to put on someone new." And, of course, "It is poetry."

They called. Let me repeat that, *they called!* Less than a week after I sent it, they called. "Did you write this?" they asked.

"Yup," I said.

"May we run it on the air?"

"I'd be thrilled!" and I was.

They ran it and called back, "Do you have anything else?"

I said, "Does a bear live in the woods?"

Lesson #35: If you shoot enough arrows in the sky, some are bound to stick.

Why did that arrow stick? Luck? Timing? The right person listened to my piece? Public radio was still new and flexible, and I didn't know I wasn't supposed to invite myself to be on such a prestigious network.

As the years went by, they ran one of my submissions every three or four weeks. They introduced me, a real agricultural person, to a primarily urban audience. Bob Edwards introduced me on the air as "Baxter Black, cowboy poet, philosopher, and former large animal veterinarian." Somewhere near the end of my first year with NPR, I was in Washington D.C. and went by their headquarters. They knew I was coming.

They had sent one of their interns out for a pastry tray in my honor. I was standing in the hall when a young woman walked in with the tray. She explained to me sincerely that the deli assured her that nothing had been cooked in animal fat and no bacon pieces were in the bagel, that no meat was allowed to touch the plate.

I thanked her with a quizzical expression. She noticed. "You're a vegetarian, right? They said you were. A large animal vegetarian."

It is easy to see why I was such a square peg in a round hole.

It was a good beginning, and funny. Then Bob Edwards, whom I had just met, introduced me to the others who were gathered and told them I thought NPR was a bunch of "pinko commies"!

His reference to "pinko commies" made me uncomfortable, but I later figured out that he had seen a letter, a solicitation piece I had done to help Nebraska Public Radio increase their membership. They were trying to get coverage into the Sandhills area of the state, a strong, well-to-do, conservative bastion of one-hundred-year-old ranching families who were so far to the right they considered Gaddafi a Presbyterian! I had appeared many times at Sandhills Cattlemen's meetings and community functions. Plus, my column and commercial radio program were widely read and listened to in the area, as they are today.

The big opposition from the Sandhills communities was public radio's perceived liberal bias. When the Nebraska Public Radio folks in Lincoln heard me on NPR, they realized, with me, they had a way to break the ice with the rural western half of the state. At Nebraska Public Radio's request, I wrote a letter to the ranching community. I addressed their objection of liberal bias directly and suggested they lighten up.

The letter must have reached all the way back to Washington D.C.! I was politically incorrect enough, or naive enough, not to recognize that it was a taboo issue at NPR. But, even today, when I'm traveling the beautiful verdant Sandhills somewhere between Carhenge and the North Platte River, I take pleasure in listening to *Weekend*  *Edition.* Maybe, I think to myself, I had a small hand in making it happen.

Lesson #36: It's hard to be what you aren't. If you can be true to yourself and true to others at the same time, you sleep better.

I met many of the public radio public figures who have been named in the programs' credits. We have remained friends. One of them was the *Morning Edition* producer, Bob Forente. He invited me into his office after I had been on a couple of years. I was obviously impressed by the operation. Its subject matter centered around New York City life and inside the Beltway politics. It was obvious I was really out of place. I had no clue how their world worked. Big city vs. "pretty ranchy." I asked him why they had included me in such an obviously sophisticated program.

He looked across the desk and said, "Because you're the only one we know from 'out there.'"

I remember thinking, "Does he mean philosophically or geographically?"

Looking back, I realize my "acceptance" was not to be taken lightly. Human nature leads people to surround themselves with people like themselves. It's not good or bad; it just is. In the late '90s I was on a national book tour. The scheduler approached one of the "primo" independent bookstores at the time, Politics and Prose in Washington D.C., to allow me to do a reading. They declined to have me in their store. The reason their publicity person gave was, "He's too rustic."

I saw the same prejudice displayed on the cover of *Newsweek* during the 2008 national election. It carried a complimentary photo of Sarah Palin, the vice presidential candidate. The caption read, "She's just folks . . . and that's the problem." I also remember the "hayseed" mantra applied to President Jimmy Carter, and the Bubba, bumpkin characterization of President Bill Clinton. In a nutshell, "they're not one of us!"

Over the years I had several producers at NPR. I would send my pieces in on reel-to-reel, then it became DAT, then CD, and then MP3. Some they would use and some they wouldn't. I rarely questioned their judgment. One that I asked them to reconsider was called the "AARP!"

It addressed the wearing of fur. I called my producer, and he said they thought it was too controversial to air. I suggested we were public radio . . . we can do controversial. He conceded and ran it.

It was a satire, funny without being mean-spirited to either side. But more importantly, it demonstrated the wide gap that separated NPR producers from the world I lived in. It was a rubbing of cultural tectonic plates: country vs. city.

AARP!
Of late there's been a modest debate
involving the wearing of fur.

There's some even swears anybody who wears it
is flawed in their character.
Yet others will fight to maintain their right
to wear what they dang well please
But the answer lies in a compromise that sets both minds at ease.

Imagine two friends at opposite ends
who meet and do lunch once a week.
Their friendship is tried when they gather outside
a Beverly Hills boutique,
"Sylvia, oh my soul, is that a mink stole?
Please tell me it's fake from goodwill!"
"Yes, Babs, it is mink, but it's not what you think,
because . . . it's designer roadkill!"

Oh, sure, you scoff, but don't blow it off,
it's the wisdom of Solomon's voice.
The perfect solution, it grants absolution
yet leaves the owner Pro Choice!
Wisdom so pure should forever endure
and percolate into your soul
So I'm the head jack of the Animal Ac-
cident Recovery Patrol!

The AARP! Which is Larry and me,
are on the road every night
To gently remind you that mess left behind you
is more than a buzzard's delight!
Carry your trowel for mammal or fowl
to collect your vehicular blooper.
In time you will find yucky's all in your mind,
no worse than a pooper scooper!

Plus, you'll be amazed how activists praise you
for doin' what you think is right
And no trapper'd object if you stopped to collect
things that go bump in the night.
But treat it with care, waste not a hare,
be sorry but don't sit and pine,
'Cause accidents happen when yer both overlappin'
the double yellow line.

So salvage your plunder and render your blunder
into a warm winter coat
And remember our motto as you know you otto,
it follows, and herein I quote,
"MAKE IT A HABIT TO PICK UP YOUR RABBIT.
DON'T LEAVE HIM TO DRY IN THE SUN.
FOR THE SAKE OF A GARMENT, RECYCLE YOUR VARMINT,
IT'S TACKY TO JUST HIT AND RUN!"

It was well received by the audience. I had seventy-plus letters (no e-mail in those days), all positive. I have routinely avoided doing political commentary on NPR. They've got millions of commentators who can do news analysis better than I can. My value was to entertain the listenership, to make them laugh. I was the sorbet between the news and political commentary.

As time went by I began to get speaking invitations from local public radio stations that carried NPR. They use my books and CDs as premium gifts during fund drives, as well as the solicitation spots I cut. I do fund-raising appearances for local stations. I try to make myself useful. Public radio has given me a window into the urban world.

They have added credibility to my otherwise fairly common self.

In 2004 NPR underwent a "reorganization," as any business does as it grows. "More professional" would be the way I would best describe it. Although they keep my picture on the website, I rarely am heard. I miss being on, as do those occasional kind folks who tell me they miss me, too. But when I consider how lucky I was to be on at all, I have no reason to say anything but eternal thanks to the producers who turned a blind eye to my "countryness," my rustic manner. Twenty years, 250-plus commentaries, all because one tape slipped through their system and stuck. One big arrow in the sky!

In a Nutshell

Having my primarily humorous commentaries on National Public Radio was one of the most satisfying, eye-opening relationships in my life. When I began, public radio listeners made me feel like I was family. That's often how they spoke of their relationship with their NPR.

I have devoted a full chapter to National Public Radio because it is one of the best examples of John Basabe's basic philosophy:

I was given a chance by NPR . . .

I found my way without a map.

They accepted me as a regular . . .

I won the game when I didn't know the rules.

And it all happened ...

because I didn't know it couldn't be done.

Lesson #37: Regarding arrows in the sky and stages in your life: Think positive, be persistent, be generous when it works, and gracious when it doesn't.

CHAPTER 7

Self-Publishing: Marketing, Promotion, Distribution, and Sales

First, a word about simply getting an agent who might success-fully sell your book to a "real" publisher. Of course, that would be the dream of 99 percent of authors! Other authors would look at you with respect; you would sell more books and make more money. Think of the anguish you would save if you eliminated the need to self-publish and market your own book.

So why doesn't everybody do that? Primarily because most unpublished authors (I would guess 95 percent) can't find an agent to represent their book. However, it is always worth a try, an arrow in the sky.

You may find on the Internet the website of AAR, the Asso-ciation of Authors Representatives, Inc. It lists many agents, their contact information, subject matter of books represented, and submission guidelines.

DISCLAIMER

It is obvious that this very book that you bought, elabo-rating self-publication and self-marketing, is actually being published by a legitimate publisher. I made the decision to seek a publisher instead of self-publishing because I felt that a "self-help" book by me would have a broader audience than my cowboy poetry books. I found my agent on the AAR website.

After searching through the literary agents listed, I selected twenty or so that included self-help, business, and humor categories as general interests. Each was sent a "form letter" on business stationery as follows:

Date and Name and address
John Doe,
Does the name Baxter Black ring a bell? Cowboy poet, former large animal veterinarian, and irregular commentator on NPR's Morning Edition*?*

Jane Doe represented Baxter since 1991—four books with Crown Publishing with 200,000 total sold. She retired this spring and recommended AAR.

Baxter has self-published and sold an additional 400,000 books (hard and soft covers) from 1980– present, plus tens of thousands of audios.

He has completed a business self-help manuscript he would like to pitch to Madison Avenue. He needs an agent with connections to business market publishers. Even though his greatest literary feat, as the New York Times *said, is as "probably the nation's most successful living poet," this is not a poetry book!*

The working title:

How to find your way without a map,

How to win the game when you don't know the rules, and

When somebody says it can't be done, what they mean is, They can't do it!

A cowboy poet's guide to the entrepreneurial universe.

If Baxter fits your client specs, please contact me at e-mail or phone.

Signed by Baxter's secretary

Three of the agents contacted us, and I visited with all three on the phone. I suspect they had an interest in me because of my successful record of book sales. I chose one.

The first thing she asked for was a book proposal. Then she explained what it was.

A book proposal is a common requirement even though I already had the full manuscript written. It often is a much more complicated and time-consuming project than the simple "synopsis and sample chapter."

There are several sample book proposals out there. Google "How to write a book proposal."

Thus, it is possible to just have an idea for a book that you want to write, and you might get an agent who will sell it to a publisher based on your book proposal. I suspect this is how it works for famous athletes, criminals, politicians, and celebrities.

But for you who are unfamiliar with the wonderful world of book publishing, I have given you a short course in taking a shot at Madison Avenue. You can lay this book down, put a marker on this page, and look up AAR. However, if you bought this book to learn how to self-publish, to improve your overall attitude, or to revitalize your entrepreneurial ventures, continue on.

Back to Self-Marketing and Distribution

Successful self-published self-marketers are a rarified group. Most of us who do it have a specific target audience. Religious books are an example, as are books on quilting, sheep diseases, stamp collectors, and in my case, the rural agricultural community.

Columnists, cooking show hosts, and radio personalities who communicate with their audience on a regular basis can usually be assured of some product sales. A couple of authors at my level who have done well enough to make a living publishing their own books are John Erickson and David Stoecklein.

John Erickson, author of the series of children's books and CDs called *Hank the Cowdog*, has catered to schools and libraries and sold several million copies. Hank is a household name in much of rural America. As you can surmise, he does more business in Texas than he does in San Francisco.

David Stoecklein is a photographer of all things cowboy. His books range in retail price from $14.95 to much higher. The cost of publishing colored photography books has often been prohibitive, but twenty-first-century technology and availability of overseas printers have allowed him to expand his market significantly. His creative marketing is fun for me to watch; he has books devoted to cowdogs, horses, regional cowboys, chaps, spurs, and cowboy cooking, and he continues to scan the cowboy horizon for new specialized subjects.

Besides talent, the outstanding quality both these men possess is dedication: meaning long hours, discipline, and a strong sense of John Basabe's self-confidence. No one has to get them up in the morning.

In my case, I have sold self-published books and what I call Crown books. Although I have sold more of the self-published copies, Crown can influence distributors and bookstores that would otherwise ignore me. But for reasons I have previously elucidated, I choose to retain ownership of my poetry.

Today my business, the Coyote Cowboy Company, distributes our self-published books and audio material directly or through several national wholesale book distributors including Ingrams and Baker and Taylor. Bookstores and libraries call these book distributors to order my books at wholesale prices. I sell my books to these companies at distributor prices, and they then turn around and sell them at wholesale prices.

The distinction between distribution and marketing should be obvious. The book distributors don't market our products;

they distribute them. But when I buy a spot in their catalogue advertising my books, then they are helping me market my product.

Marketing Is Promotion Plus Sales

Amazon, on the other hand, by offering book information with reviews online, promotes and sells product. Bookstores do book signings, advertising, and shelf placement displays to promote and sell books. They buy direct from us at the wholesale price and then market them to customers at the retail price.

Doing a radio interview about your new book is promotion. Placing your book display on the checkout counter is marketing.

In addition to Ingrams, Amazon, and other major chain bookstores, we use a variety of methods and sources to distribute, market, promote, and sell the majority of our books, CDs, and DVDs.

Around the country there are a few well-established regional independent distributors who have a customer list they maintain and care for. Their list may include feed stores; curio shops; Betty's Books in Baker City, Oregon; Brighton Feed and Farm Supply in Brighton, Colorado; and Wimpy's One Stop in Olton, Texas!

For the self-published author, these distributors can be very beneficial.

Over the years we have found many ways to market our books at wholesale and retail levels. They include magazine advertising, the Internet, western stores, smaller independent bookstores, at public appearances, book signings, trade shows, RFD-TV, local public radio affiliates as premium gifts, mail order, interviews, and trade-outs with newspapers carrying my column. An inventive marketer can create his own opportunities.

Lesson #38: If you are easily discouraged, vain, or sensitive to rejection, then entrepreneurism is not for you. Stick to a job that offers company insurance and a retirement package.

So, you decide to self-publish. Find a local printing company, let them help you figure out how to meld your dream manuscript into a book that they are capable of printing and you can afford. Don't mortgage the house to have it printed. Be smart. A run of 1,500 books is cheaper per book than a run of 500. But if you can't sell them at any price or don't have that many relatives to give them to, even 500 is a lot of books to keep in the closet!

Lesson #39: Regarding your first self-published book or CD, don't worry about it making or losing money.

Know how much you are willing to invest (and lose, if need be), close your eyes, and do it! Get help when you need it. Don't be extravagant in the size of your order and stick with a soft cover.

Now you've got a box of thirty-two books in the trunk of your car. Where's your first stop? The local feed store, western store, co-op, bookstore, tourist trap, or if it is a book on barbecue recipes, try the cafe! Any retail outlet that looks promising. Remember, their only interest in selling your book is for them to get a piece of the action!

If your book is about people from your community, try the historical society or museum. Somewhere, sometime, someone will buy your book. They will see it and buy it, and you will become an official author!

When you are placing your books in a retail store, you tell them the suggested retail price and charge them wholesale, which is usually 60 percent of retail. Be prepared to leave your books with them on consignment (they pay you only for those they sell). This is fair if you are a new author. They are lending you the space to sell your book. Thank the manager, autograph the books, and write it down!

Sometimes it seems pretentious, but offer the manager a free autographed copy. If, by some chance, someone in the store reads it and likes it, you have a local, vocal recommendation! That, my friends, is hard to beat.

Next step is the local paper in your area. See if they will review it. Send review copies to magazines and trade papers that might relate to your content. Speak to the Rotary Club, go to the poetry gathering. Give them away to anybody who might have influence. Leave a copy in the beauty salon, barbershop, doctor's office, nursing home, school library . . . keep scattering them until one day you hear someone say, "Hey, I read your book. I really like it!"

Be creative about getting your book in front of folks, and don't be afraid to ask for the manager.

Lesson #40: It is always best to be able to make your sales presentation directly to the person who makes the purchasing decisions.

When the first box of thirty-two is gone, put another one in the trunk and keep pitching!

The mad, mad world of technology has made us easily available to the world. It has broadened our marketing area exponentially. In the book *The World Is Flat*, author Thomas Friedman makes the point that because of satellites and the Internet we in Buffalo, Wyoming, or Buffalo, New York, can do business with customers in Goondawindi, Queensland, Australia, or Lahore, Pakistan.

You can use your own web page or YouTube, Facebook, Twitter, eBay, or Google account to promote your product and grant access to your customers. These services will do nothing but improve the opportunities for entrepreneurs.

We use our web page extensively. We try to keep it fresh and updated with appealing, entertaining features, our itinerary, product availability, and how to reach us. It is difficult to place a value on the cost of maintaining a web page. It is hard to evaluate its return on investment.

Web pages are valuable, but they are expensive. The same for computers, which consume money and time like piranhas! But they give us access to the world and more information than we can possibly use in a lifetime. They have become as essential for life as bottled water and disposable diapers.

A simple web page, YouTube channel, or a Facebook account with contact information would be a basic beginning. The next step for you is to entice the buyer to buy your books with your promotion skills. Finally you must offer them a place to make the transaction: i.e., your web page, a store, distributor, eBay, your phone number, e-mail, or address.

So much of the cyber world operates with expectations of little or no money exchange. And yet, to establish and maintain your electronic or physical store can be quite costly.

Make sure your business sales justify the whistles and bells you put on your electronic train.

Lesson #42: Every contact you make about your book is another arrow in the sky. And though it is an inefficient way to get your product out, it is a legitimate marketing method. Remember, there may be a Tom Robbins waiting for you somewhere!

In a Nutshell

This is a short chapter about the hardest part of self-publishing. It's like a sea turtle laying eggs in the middle of I-10—anywhere on I-10—and hoping one will hatch!

Every step of the way toward getting your book into the hands of a reader is fraught with indifference, drought, theft, hurricanes, carelessness, amnesia, poor lighting, illiteracy, and a steady, gradual loss of page by page when left in the campground outhouse.

But you were warned not to expect a crowd of thousands and an invitation to be on C-SPAN2's BookTV the first week.

Your saving grace is, if you've had enough experience punching cows, making sales calls, starting tractors at 20 degrees below zero, putting kids through school, and having bones broken by bad buckers to write a book full of poetry, marketing your book will be as easy as peeling an apple with an electric sander!

Fill your quiver and fire that first arrow . . . you're already half-way there!

P.S. This chapter is a specific approach to self-marketing books, but it can easily be extrapolated to other ideas, products, or services an entrepreneur may be attempting to market.

CHAPTER 8

Marketing Outrageously

I have often heard, and I believe, that the easiest person to sell something to . . . is a salesman!

Climbing in the car of a realtor, pharmaceutical salesperson, or stockbroker, you often see stacks of self-help CDs, inspirational bumper stickers, and good luck tokens.

There are a handful of people who are able to make a living without having to sell themselves or their product, be it their singing ability, invention, latest book, or good looks.

For the rest of us, we can either learn to sell ourselves, or hire someone else to do it. Some of the most successful combinations are those of people who can do something saleable with another who can sell their product.

Authors, performers, inventors, painters, tire manufacturers, and politicians can hire publicity agents, lawyers, gallery owners, advance men, ad agencies, pundits, ghostwriters, joke writers, scriptwriters, speechwriters, and makeup persons to "sell" the product or skill even though they themselves can't paint, act, play football, run for office, or write their own autobiography.

Although this book is primarily aimed at the entrepreneur himself, you may be the person who sells the entrepreneur's skills or product. If you are doing it on a commission, then you are throwing your lot in with the gambler. To wit:

Lesson #43: A good middleman is often the difference between a talent who still has a day job at Walgreens and one singing in Carnegie Hall.

If you can't sell yourself as well as the middleman "selling" you, pay up, don't resent him, and let him do it! For the rest of us who aren't in a position to have a middleman, I often see the spouse and/or family help with the promotion. When it works, it is a blessing. When it doesn't, cease and desist to save the marriage!

I have been modestly successful selling myself and so am susceptible to self-help books. The kind I particularly find useful are about marketing trends and demographics, success stories from businesspeople who have done well, and the occasional spectacular title that makes me open the book!

Lesson #44: Bookstores and newsstands are full of self-help books and CDs for businesspeople and salespeople. If you can glean one idea to improve your attitude, presentation, or management, it's worth $19.95!

Two books have had a significant influence in my business. The first is *The Solid Gold Mailbox* by Walter Weintz first published in 1987. To put this in perspective, it was written and applied to my business pre-Internet. The book proposed to show the reader how to increase his or her mail-order business.

The claim to fame of the author was that he invented the technique of enclosing a penny in each solicitation envelope. It was avant-garde at the time.

My company sent out our first Christmas mailing in October of 1984. It was a fold-over one-page sheet offering our first books and cassettes. The mail-order list had been built from business cards I routinely collected from folks when I was on the road. We did our flyer like most can imagine: some illustration, reviews, prices, address, and phone number.

We progressed, though our presentation did not get much fancier. The mailing list grew (more about that later). In 1989 I discovered *The Solid Gold Mailbox* and took it hook, line, and sinker! In the book are many specific techniques to help you market by mail. Some of those we still use in our marketing. For instance, he promoted the "Hot Potato" or "Action Device."

Over the years for large mailings (between ten thousand and fifteen thousand), we have included silly or fun extras such

as decals, jerky, bookmarks, popcorn, and duck feathers just to name a few.

On the front of the mailing is notice of a discount, *Buy Two . . . Get One Free!* with the enclosed coupon. The coupon was the hot potato. The action device must first get them to open the envelope.

Once you've got them "inside," the next step is to get them to place an order. The promotional piece shows them what the product is. If they are interested, they see that the coupon has an expiration date.

The logic is that if you want to get the "Buy Two Get One Free" offer you have to send in the coupon. The object is to get people to place the order right away, not wait and possibly mislay the coupon.

One of the recommendations of *The Solid Gold Mailbox* is that the special offer has to be real, specific to the mailer, related to the coupon, and it has to be a true bargain.

Lesson #45: If you expect repeat business, your offer has to be a "genuine good deal."

If you watch the barrage of "direct marketing" television ads that promote clever, apparently useful, "Why didn't I think of that"?" products, you see how it works. If you think that you need a pair of the wraparound sunglasses that fit over your eyeglasses and the youthful couple in Miami modeling them proclaim, "I've never seen sunglasses as clear as these!" you might be thinking, "But $19.95 for a pair of sunglasses is a lot," and then, and then! They offer a second pair of night vision wraparound sunglasses! Absolutely *free*! Glasses that cut the glare from oncoming traffic, *plus* a magnificent carrying case that attaches to the sun visor! A $45.00 value for only $19.95 plus shipping and handling (usually $7.95). So, a genuine good deal is in the eye of the beholder. That is the test of your product.

Over the years the Internet and our 800 number have drawn away from an actual order placed in the mail, so we still send the coupon in the mailer in October, but when they order on the phone or online, we accept and honor the discount. However, we still retain the limited-time requirement to get the discount. It runs out Christmas Eve.

Another technique that we adopted and still use in our mail-order flyers is the personal-introduction letter on the top. And it is a long one. In all Mr. Weintz's extensive mail-order statistics, the longer the introductory letter the more orders you receive. The irony is, people tell you they don't read junk mail, so you would think the shorter the letter the better. Not so for mail-order people.

However, the letter must, as Mr. W. says, "have something to say, and said with some skill."

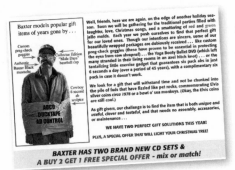

In our case we try to make the letter personally friendly from us, me and the people who work for me, be clever if possible, uplifting, and in the spirit of the holidays.

Why send the flyers out in October?

Lesson #46: Timing has a lot to do with a doctor's, plumber's, or mechanic's availability. "You got here just in time! I have a house payment due tomorrow!"

Timing is a factor in sending out your mailing. We specifically promote our products as Christmas gifts and send our mailer appropriately. Therefore October and November are when we receive our greatest response. But in Mr. W's book describing generic mail orders, the greatest months are, in order, January (yes, January!), February, October, September, August, and March. So you are not necessarily limited to the holidays. Nor are you limited to just one mailing!

He also discussed the importance of the mailing list you have compiled or bought. Obviously it would be beneficial if those who received it knew of you or were interested in the subject of your product.

He also stressed the appearance of the mailing. To that end, for the last twenty years we have used professional graphic artists to produce our mailer, or flyers, as we call them.

Back to the mailing list. If you are starting from scratch, you need to refer yourself to the many books, including *The Solid Gold Mailbox*, that can guide you. There are companies online that sell a variety of specific mailing lists. For instance, lists can be sorted by sex, age, geographic location, hobbies, vocations, musical ability, education, and/or income.

On a less expansive level, you can use Yellow Pages, directories of professions, association memberships, your high school annual, or do a library or Internet search. In the past we have bought or discovered some of these specific mailing lists: Farm Bureau members from the state of Kentucky, women who belong to the American Quarter Horse Association, FFA graduates who have attained the American Farmer degree, cowboys who have actually read a book! These lists have been spotty in their success, but each year we seem to think up another "classification of the population" that sounds promising. Arrows in the sky.

My experience has been with a much more select list. We have accumulated, refined, and regularly updated our list over many years. Today our list includes approximately 10,000 flyers to retail buyers and 1,000 to wholesale companies.

Lesson #47: For a mailing list to be effective and efficient, it must be kept as current as your parole officer's cell phone number!

The bulk of our mailing list consists of people who have previously ordered, new friends I have met and added to the list, those who have bought from us on the Internet, and new purchasers who found us through a magazine, the radio, or television. Computerizing our orders, names, addresses, and products bought helps us keep our mailing list clean!

The costly procedure of having the undeliverable flyers returned to the sender is also worth it. People move, change addresses, get divorced, and die, but they keep getting your flyers! When it's costing a dollar apiece to send each one and it ends up in the dead letter box, they create a pretty big hole in the bottom of your boat.

We examine our mailing list annually, and those who have not ordered for the last five years are deleted. The advantage of a well-tended list is a higher percent return. In the last twenty years we have rarely fallen below a 10 percent return.

That can be compared to the blanket nonspecific mailers that consider a 1 percent return good. The key to their success is in large numbers. It is a perfect example of arrows in the sky, a marketing method you will hear me praise. But I cannot afford blanket mailing lists. I shoot for a smaller, more susceptible segment of potential buyers.

I have been able to delineate my "base," and even though I still shoot lots of arrows in the sky, at least I know which way to point. This applies to other facets of my business as well as the sale of books and CDs.

Lesson #48: It helps to define your audience for marketing purposes. Regarding mine, I tell people I have a narrow following, but it's deep.

In November 2003 I was speaking at the Tulare California Expo and Museum. I noticed that they had renovated their museum. It no longer reminded you of your uncle's machine shed in February. It looked bright and airy. There were children playing with agricultural learning tools. Pictures, well-preserved refurbished farm equipment, and audio and visual aids enhanced the design and intent.

I complimented the director on the spectacular change. He handed me a book. "Here," he said. "This is how we did it."

The book was called *Marketing Outrageously*. I read it on the plane ride home, and it was invigorating! I ordered five of the books, which was the intention of the author, of course. But that is to his credit. He gave me some basic marketing ideas.

When the new books came, I personalized each to five people whose minds I admired. In each book I put a $100 bill with the offer that if they would read the book and come to my meeting next Tuesday for lunch, they could keep the bookmark. Four of those people work for me, and the other was my clever sister-in-law.

"What can we do to improve our business?" was the question on the table.

The abiding principle of marketing outrageously that still guides me is demonstrated in this example:

One of the first applications came when we were discussing how to get more publications to carry my column. We picked out a list of newspapers from Gebbie Press based on my "popularity" in the region, proximity to other publications that carried my column, where our radio program was carried, the strength of the surrounding agricultural community, the number of people on our mailing list in the area, and my gut instinct.

A special mailer of approximately one hundred was to go to the editors of small to medium weekly or daily newspapers. In my mind these men and women are usually civic-minded, literary workaholics who never catch up and are always fighting to keep the paper in the black, so to speak. Also please recall my earlier observation that "it is the editor's job to keep me out of print."

So far so good, but where does marketing outrageously come in?

We decided to send each editor a first-class, heavy-duty coffee cup. I envisioned that their morning cup of coffee was one of the few pleasures they had each day. On it we printed some clever "baxterisms" such as "Editors Exorcize Your Writes," "Write or Wong."

We all agreed that the cup was spectacular (cost $5 each!), but we needed something more, something to inspire them to read the letter offering my column. But what to put in the coffee cup? Marketing outrageously, we went around the table suggesting possibilities; a bag of expensive exotic coffee—no, that's not outrageous, that won't leave an impression. Candy? Nuts? "Come on!" I exhorted. "Think outside the box, think outrageously!"

"A basketball, lemon, bag of charcoal, a monkey, a fish!" Suddenly everyone laughed. I looked around the table. "A fish!" They all were laughing. "That won't work, but it's hilarious!"

Lesson #49: Regarding marketing outrageously, when searching for something to attract the attention of a buyer, it's the comment or item that makes you laugh but is so ridiculous on the surface that no one thinks it will work . . . that is exactly the one that will work! Obviously, if it's funny but vulgar, cruel, or too politically incorrect, you must use your judgment. Remember consumers, clients, and fans have a lifetime memory of being offended!

As the laughter subsided, the conversation continued, "Besides, it would never fit . . . A guppy might . . . You mean a real fish . . . How 'bout a plastic fish . . . Or a minnow in a plastic bag? Ooooh, uugg . . . How 'bout tuna?"

Everybody laughed again, but said, "Tuna is funny, but won't it smell bad before it reaches them in the mail?"

"No, not tuna salad, you couldn't send tuna salad . . . but tuna in the can . . . don't they make some army ration tuna cans that are small?"

We found little two-ounce cans of tuna at Safeway that fit, with room to spare, inside our magnificent cup. We decorated the shipping box we sent it in with fishy come-ons. The letter inside was filled with puns and allusions to Pisces.

My experience with editors had been that they don't have much time to write or respond to solicitations. Out of the one hundred we sent, we received over twenty whimsical, not unkind letters remarking on our absurdity and good humor. I ran into one of the editors five years later. He still had the coffee cup, which he was using, and the can of tuna was a paperweight/objet d' art on his desk!

Lesson #50: 'Tis sweet to be remembered. Entrepreneurs, salespeople, and employees all appreciate feedback. Especially if it is encouraging!

Oh, and I think we sold one newspaper. At $10 a week it will take approximately two years to pay for the ad campaign!

Another example of marketing outrageously: In the years following September 11, 2001, the government was involved in disseminating radio spots that dealt with preparedness, should another natural disaster or terrorist attack occur. States and counties were funded to keep their communities informed. I was approached by a county supervisor in Colorado to write and record some preparedness spots. They concerned themselves with educating the public to have a plan that the whole family would know, i.e., where the kids should go, whom to call, which routes to take out of town, what to do in a medical emergency, how to be ready if the power and phones went out, etc.

I wrote him several demo samples at no charge. He liked what I had done, and we made the deal. I asked him if all the states had programs like Colorado. The answer was yes. He furnished me with a list of both the directors of the state preparedness committee and the medical associate directors from each state. The director dealt with the money; the medical associate director, with the training of community volunteers, EMTs, hospital responders, policemen, and firefighters. They staged emergency situations to test their disaster readiness.

We had our marketing outrageously meeting and came up with a mailer to the approximately one hundred people who might have some say in running emergency preparedness commercials on the radio.

Lesson #51: First they have to open the envelope!

We addressed each plain manila envelope to the specific "bureaucrat" on the list by name. Then we designed a white sticky label containing the "imprint" of a big rubber stamp that said, IMPORTANT COWBOY DISASTER INFORMATION!

When they pulled out the contents, the first thing they found was a dramatic 4 x 6 photo of me holding my horse. He was looking one direction and I was looking the other. Each photo was inscribed, ON THE LOOKOUT FOR DANGER!

When they lifted off the photo, there was a neatly folded shoulder-length plastic sleeve normally used by large animal veterinarians to rectally palpate cows and horses. A Post-It note was attached to each one with the handwritten message, "When a latex glove is not enough!" Beneath that was the solicitation letter.

Lesson #52: Somehow you must inspire them to read the message enclosed.

We have come to believe that to close the sale you must talk to or e-mail the specific person who makes the decisions. In the case of complicated sales pitches like these, each one must be handled separately. Each state had a budget. Each had different requirements. Each had to be convinced that what we could do was useful and fit their needs.

Over the next several months we did spots for three more states. It was a very successful operation for us. I think the single biggest contributing factor was that one state had used us previously. We had the best reference you could get, a fellow director to recommend us. He could also be a ready scapegoat if it didn't work.

Lesson #53: A solid positive reference, be it the buyer's co-professional or competitor, is better than a jalapeño hot fudge sundae!

"I agree, Mr. President, I should have known better. I mean a cowboy poet? But Jeff up there in Colorado vouched for him and, well, what does he know!"

The marketing outrageously mentality is now part of our regular thinking, be it a fun clever graphic art letter, envelope, page, package, or the continuing designs for our web page, the answering machine on the business phone, our Christmas flyer, smaller mailers soliciting for the column, the radio program, or to produce commercials for others or our own television show on RFD-TV.

Brainstorm, think outside the box, and find what's funny, or touching, or rings a bell. *The Solid Gold Mailbox* stressed the use of a hot potato, something inside the mailer that will stimulate an immediate opening.

One popular "hot potato" we incorporate is chocolate. It has to be used during cool weather. One of our regular *exclusive* mailing lists for the Christmas market includes those who buy 12 to 120 books for employees or customers. It is our Gold Label offer. The books contain a bookplate with the name or logo of the buyer and often are personally autographed to names on his list.

Our Gold Label promotion includes special "chocolate bars" made to relate to the name of the book or CD. For *Horseshoes, Cowsocks & Duckfeet*, the chocolate was a cow patty with a duck track in it! *The World According to Baxter Black* had a chocolate piece that looked like the Earth globe with a crack in it!

The Gold Label list contains fifty or so special buyers. The solicitation they receive contains the friendly letter with details, an autographed sample copy of the new product, and the piece of chocolate. Out-of-pocket actual expense for each mailer can run from $6 to $12. We routinely get a better than 50 percent return order. We are always on the lookout for other potential Gold Label possibilities.

In a Nutshell

Whether you are a plumber, horse trainer, whittler, scrap iron collector, one-man owner-operator of an espresso kiosk, western store owner, or freelance nuclear physicist looking to sell your services or product, you have many of the same hurdles in common with this cowboy poet.

Each entrepreneur has to evaluate his customer base, devise a way to get the message to that base, and then convince that customer to buy. To sell vacuum cleaners you need to get in the door, to sell by mail order or e-mail you've got to get them to open the envelope, and to sell by magazine, radio, or television you have to convince the reader, listener, or viewer:

To remember ("What was that 800 number again?")

To change locations ("Somebody go find me a paper and pencil!")

To write a note, call on the telephone, or fire up a computer and find a web page.

The hardest of these three is "convincing them to remember." Handy devices that help them remember are a visual image, a catchy phrase, and/or a memorable phone or web address. Make it easy to remember. Allow yourself to be easy to find. No odd spellings, no unpronounceable names, and, with some exceptions, keep it short and informative: billsplumbing.com, prettyflowers.com, irs.org. If Geico insurance had been lizard insurance or caveman insurance, they would have needed to run only half as many of those cute commercials simply because no one is sure how to spell Geico, as witnessed by my spell-check, which just underlined Geico three times. They might as well have named it Gecko!

Chapter 9

How to Control Your Tech Addiction

In my early years of working with the Simplot Livestock Company, I instigated the incorporation of computerized systems into the cattle feeding operation. I had seen its management value in my previous livestock company job and was convinced that it would help us feed cattle more efficiently.

It was a hard sell in the mid-'70s. After doing the preliminary research, I arranged a "sales pitch" presentation to the feedlot managers. I invited two technical sales reps from the computer company to do the talking.

It was a hot afternoon in the un-air-conditioned lunchroom at the Caldwell feedlot. The tech reps talked for an hour, showing us graphs and charts, giving thorough explanations of how this modern high technology would put us on the cutting edge. The speaker concluded by saying, "We can give you a stack of information that reaches the ceiling, we can give it to you almost overnight [it was in the punch card days], and we can give it to you in triplicate!"

His oration clung in the heavy air for a moment, then Glenn McQ, the cattle foreman, rose to his feet and said, "I don't care how much information you can give us, as long as it's on smooth paper!"

One of the miraculous qualities of cyberspace and computer technology is its seemingly bottomless cornucopia of information. It's like holding a plastic cup underneath Niagara Falls!

Lesson #54: Although computers can barrage us with more facts, opinions, and gossip than we can possibly absorb, the key to giving it value is your ability to sort the snowflakes from the blizzard.

Those of you with carpal tunnel already know this!

For the sake of clarification I am going to separate "accounting" functions from "marketing" functions. The first, "accounting," I think of as falling in three services.

Technology has allowed us to gather, organize, and therefore make use of data we collect. Automatic billing, collating, keeping inventory, sorting, credit cards, and banking are examples of #1, "number crunching." In this classification I include the calculation function that takes the data gathered and calculates the trajectory of a missile.

It also allows #2, "communication," to and from places near and far that previously was never deemed possible. E-mail, You-Tube, MySpace, and Facebook now make it simple to conduct business, diplomacy, war, and pleasure through cyberspace as easily as we could with someone next door.

Technology in area #3, "research," has placed a universe of information at your fingertips. Computers have replaced encyclopedias, textbooks, telephone lines, newspapers, dictionaries, song sheets, classrooms, astronomy and astrology magazines, and a multitude of information sources that were heretofore essential for gathering data on the topic of your choice. You can look up everything from the total greenhouse gases produced by landfills in the United States last year to booking tomorrow's airline flights.

It is possible to place a value on these services and procedures. We pay phone bills, employee salaries, and computer hardware expenses that can be quantified. We have a way of proving to ourselves that we are getting our money's worth from the technology we pay for.

There are some drawbacks, or at least precautions when using the Internet to seek information. For instance, the time entanglement trap one can fall into in search of an obscure fact. This is due in part to the marbles you have to sort through to find the blue-eyed one with the Masonic insignia on the iris, and, of course, the time spent looking at all the other marbles because they were so pretty!

Lesson #55: The Internet can be a distracting, addictive habit and a voracious thief of time.

Another factor that wafts through cyberspace like the unpleasant smell of a wet dog in the back of your car is that the information can often be inaccurate. Source verification or confirmation from a second source can be a wise idea if you smell something fishy.

Lesson #56: Don't believe anything you hear, half of what you see, and if it sounds too good on the Internet, frisk the prisoner.

But the accounting functions of technology have allowed and continue to allow humans to advance our civilization at an astonishing pace.

The value of technological services in the "marketing" portion of our business is more difficult to evaluate. There are many examples in my company where we use technology beyond the '60s methods of the post office and the telephone, to solicit business.

It can be something as simple as using e-mail to do a direct mailing. For instance, I had written a patriotic piece for Memorial Day 2008 during the Iraq War called "Lucky to Be an American." It ran on my RFD-TV television program. It was well-received. Complimentary e-mails began arriving asking for DVD copies and permission to use it.

Most of the requests stated that they had received it as an e-mail. A little digging revealed that it had been posted on YouTube by more than one person (however, not by us because we did not use YouTube at that time). People were lifting my piece from its regular television airing onto their computer and e-mailing it to their friends. My untechnical mind began to wonder how could someone else be putting my material up on their own site and distributing it?

"That's the Internet, Farm Boy," explained my webmaster. "People can use your name, your products, your thoughts, your material, and your identity with virtually no retribution. You have no privacy. The world is flat. You are standing out in the open with no cover for Internet snipers! Once you have signed up, you are fair game."

Lesson #57: Warning: The line between privacy, plagiarism, property rights, piracy, plunder, and

propaganda, vs. professional and personal pro-
priety is blurred on the Internet. It is truly caveat
emptor.

Regarding the dissemination of "Lucky," many requests to use it were from veterans, soldiers on duty, and patriotic Americans. I was flattered, and we did not charge for its use. We had a marketing outrageously meeting to figure out how we could gain some control of our program now that it had developed its own momentum. We decided to create our own YouTube account and place "*Lucky*," as well as three others, online. Then we put a link from our YouTube videos to our website.

The requests continued to pour in over the summer, but we really had no way to measure how it affected our business. Count e-mails? Phone calls? Letters?

At year's end we had proceeded on to marketing our fall product and were preoccupied with sales and shipping. "Lucky" stepped into the background. In January I asked for the annual summary of website hits, visits, pages, etc., for review. January through May held steady at 320–380K hits. June slipped to 266,000 as usually happens in our business during the summer. July was 293,000, then August shot up to 588,000! Then it fell back down in the 350s for autumn and not until our fall mailing and Christmas season did the visits rise and then they hit 797,000.

We puzzled about that August spike and concluded that it was the result of our new YouTube link, primarily from "Lucky" to our web page. It was responsible for doubling our hits for a period of four weeks! Visits and page views were up a third.

So the question is "Was it good for business?"

Webmaster cost: $45 an hour plus time screening e-mails, responding, mailing copies, hours spent by employees, and miscellany. The DVD production cost was defrayed by sponsors on RFD-TV.

The answer to the question: Yes, it was good for business. It is enormously flattering for an author or entertainer to be liked. I have an admiration and respect for those who serve in the armed forces. I have received tokens of their thanks that are invaluable to me. When the general uses your poem to address the troops, it's very humbling. It is possible that I received a speaking invitation or two from those who became new fans after reading "Lucky."

But did we make any money? Much harder to evaluate the effect of the "Lucky" run. Did it stimulate book sales? Did it bring people to my live shows? To my web page, column, radio, or television programs? I'd have to conclude, maybe.

A good marketing ad agency person would say that it increased visibility, therefore my "'fan base,' therefore was good for business."

This actual experience is skewed by the fact that we virtually made the product available at no charge. If "Lucky" had been something more commercial that I could have priced like we do CDs, DVDs, or a printed poster, then it would be easier to evaluate its direct value as a product and not just a promotional enterprise. Yet, maybe not. Because if I was trying to sell something that a pirate had taken from me and put on his own website, YouTube account, or Facebook page, and was giving it away free, it would be a losing proposition.

Just ask any Nashville recording artist whose record sales have plummeted since the Internet has made product available at little to no charge. Or ask any reporter whose newspaper went under because they somehow thought if they published it on the Internet, people would still buy their print version. Or any book author or independent bookstore that is battling Internet sources.

Businesses have spending centers like research, product development, manufacturing, shipping, marketing, and sales. "Lucky" and my web page, YouTube, e-mailings, shipping, and labor costs would, in this case, be charged against that fuzzy, hard-to-define classification called marketing and promotion.

Lesson #58: You can't blame a fan for buying a discounted book or CD. You can't blame a fan for downloading your material that someone else put up for grabs. You can't not shop at WalMart.

A year later I put three patriotic pieces on one DVD including, "Lucky to Be an American," "Grandpa Tommy Saved the World," and "The Flag." We priced the package at $20. We were able to get the e-mail addresses of all the VFWs in the United States. My crew put together a first-class solicitation. It included a downloadable sample and an appropriate "verbiage."

My thought was that they could use them, these DVD pieces, on holidays, meeting openings, and occasions where a patriotic theme might be applicable. We received zero responses. We are still sending out the occasional e-mail or paper copy of "Lucky." It has a life of its own. I guess if they wanted the DVD version, they'd just copy it off the Internet for nothing.

My company began building our first web page in 2000. It progressed steadily. By 2004 we were set up for customers to order online. My television show, which is a weekly three-minute commentary, went on the air in November 2005 on satellite network RFD-TV.

In 2005, Denver had two major newspapers; only 60 percent of the public had cell phones; Garth Brooks had sold over 100 million CDs; texting, Blackberries, iPods, and cell phone cameras were still novel ideas; Facebook was just a year old; Twitter did not yet exit; Saddam Hussein was in custody; 897 soldiers were killed in the war on terror, and *Crash* won the Academy Award for Best Picture.

I thought, from the positive public response I was receiving, that I would be able to market my new TV programs on our web page. People could buy and download them from there. We debated how much to charge for each program: $12 or $10? We had high hopes. It was a huge undertaking. It took us many months to finally get the product up and available. We started at $5 each, three for $10.

One could see a sample program at no charge. Then we placed all twenty-six (one year's production) up on the web page. Each one had a picture and a two-line description of the story. I sat back and waited. I'm still waiting! A rough estimate, in five years we have had 230 of them downloaded. Gross: $1,150.

I was hoping with the popularity of the show it would become a nice profit center.

I was wrong.

The hits on the website continued at a nice number, as they still do. We made an effort from 2006 to 2009 at keeping the home page fresh, changing the offering and appeal monthly. We had specials running all the time. Holidays were emphasized. We had several features including photos of my road travels, pictures of pets named Baxter, favorite CD cuts, my weekly column—it was a fine website. Our webmaster came in several hours a week to keep it current. It was a costly operation in both time and money.

In 2009 the nation was in a serious economic downturn. One of the many facets of our business we reexamined for profitability was the web page. Looking at the number of hits per category, we realized that some of them received less than 10 percent of the regular viewership. I chose to discontinue those sections that were poorly visited. It included ones I liked, such as photos I took of my road trips with lots of people whom I wanted to recognize, a section where I recommended CDs and books that I had been sent. Other features such as the weekly column that had a better showing we have continued.

We are still on the lookout for items that will bring return viewers back to our website on a regular basis. The objective, other than promotion, is to stimulate purchases of books, CDs, and DVDs, and notify the viewers of new product.

The website, as I have shown, is an efficient way to accomplish the process of selling our product. Customers order and pay online. We can evaluate that quantitatively. It continues to creep up annually as a part of total sales. It encourages us to continue to invest in improving our product catalogue, its presentation, and ease of online ordering. I feel comfortable about its value.

But how does one evaluate a website as a marketing tool? Do a survey of all the orders you receive? All the sales you make? Once people found your website, did it tend to increase the size of the order per visit? Did your home page lead a first-timer to look at your product pages? Does it stimulate watching my television program? Will it make the crowds at my live shows bigger? In other words, does it pay its own way?

My answer is that a web page can be a good part of the marketing, promotion, and sales portion of your business. It is often at its best when it is used as the first referral in your advertisement or public appearance or the back of your book.

"You ran out of books," they say disappointedly. "No sweat," says I. "You can find it at baxterblack.com!"

In a small entrepreneurial operation, sometimes even a one-man show, a website can serve as your office. No matter where you are, it can show potential customers around your possibilities. Then if they like what they see, they can find your phone number or e-mail address and make contact.

You can do good business with a catchy, professional home page, whether you do in-home sewing, teach welding, or are an authority on the Russian poet Pushkin.

Lesson #59: As a marketing tool, do not think of your web page as the NASA ad agency or the bat cave. Think of it as someone who works for you, really likes you, knows what you do, and can answer the phone pleasantly. Expect neither miracles nor confusion from your web page. Treat it as a helpful receptionist.

In a Nutshell

Technology is already defining our new century. Things we marveled at ten years ago have disappeared and been replaced by even more capable productivity in smaller and smaller packages. Computers, telephones, cameras, calculators, surgical instruments, implants, a never-ending stream of smaller, better, more powerful, more efficient, and cheaper . . . yes, cheaper improvements.

An entrepreneur's greatest asset and advantage is his mind. Minds that God gave us that invented or thought up everything we know, including technology. Technology that is smaller, better, more efficient, and will probably be obsolete before the inventor's next birthday!

Albert Einstein, an acknowledged mathematical mental entre-

preneur, was said to have been able to picture the concepts in his mind, to see them function long before he went back to put the equations on the blackboard. He was criticized for not writing down all of the basic equations. He didn't bother because they were clear to him and he was miles down the road, calculating the unknown.

It is typical of "out of the box" thinkers. They were pondering how to survive in zero gravity before man had ever flown.

Technology can tell us how many people in the country can read. It can tell us how many self-help books are sold each year. Statistics can tell us how many people are interested in starting their own business. But, if you are one of the latter, inside your brain, in the middle of the night, the idea is stirring that it is hard to buy a good chocolate chip cookie, that there must be a greener way to package bottles of water, or why can't somebody invent some design that will keep dust from building up on the rear window of your SUV.

These ideas are created beyond the realm of technology. They stir and mix like many colors in a paint can. They stew, bubble, ferment, and steam. They are as unique and uncountable as each person's DNA.

Lesson #60: Technology cannot help an entrepreneur with no imagination.

CHAPTER 10
The Act of Self-Publishing— Preparing Your Manuscript

If you've already got an agent and/or publisher, you may skip forward to chapter 11.

It is only fair to mention that there are university presses, specialty book publishers, cookbook publishers, exercise publishers, even some that specialize in poetry! You can actually buy self-help books that explain how to approach these publishers. There are books full of lists of these specialty presses, literary agents, and an Internet full of ideas, but the odds that you will get your book published (and published means paid for!) by one of them are not in your favor. You are outside the system. And that is what this book is about, that's what the title means. Remember, it is the job of the program director, the editor, and the publisher to keep you off the air and out of print. Do not take it personally.

When you decide to self-publish, the first step is to prepare a manuscript. You must have something in hand to show them to get printing estimates.

Lesson #61: First things first . . . Can you type? Are you computer literate? If the answer is no, then you need to find a friend.

I will confine my comments here to books that are collections of stories, anecdotes, or poems because that is my experience. Obviously, if you have written a novel, the editing would be a different process although marketing information is still applicable.

It is likely that you have your collection of poems or fictional or historical anecdotes in a notebook or a file folder in your top drawer. They may be handwritten. I suggest you make a copy of everything you're thinking of including in your first book right away. They have a value to you and people who care about you. Keep a copy of your originals in another place. If you have done it all on the computer, make a backup copy as well. Imagine your house burning or being picked up by a tornado while you're vacationing in Casa Grande.

Think about the order of how you would like your poems to appear in your book. A technique I use is to make a list of all the poems and/or short stories to be included in the book and "grade them" A, B, or C. The grade is my own evaluation of their popularity, with A being the best. I also mark whether they are serious or funny (S or F).

Then I draw a large horizontal-vertical cross on a piece of paper, dividing it into four quarters. With the intimate knowledge of each poem that only the author has, I begin filling each quarter. I lovingly place As in each quarter, Bs in each one, and Cs in each one. I also interspace the serious ones with the funny ones.

If your book is a historical collection of your grandpa's life, then it will probably be in chronological order. There is an art to organizing your book. It is what editors do for money.

The objective is to make the book an enjoyable read. One poem or story should lead into the next. I try to avoid sandwiching a heart-wrenching piece where the dad loses the ranch between a story about a cowboy getting bucked off with his pants down around his knees or one with me pushing a uterine prolapse back in with my head!

"WELL, DON'T STOP NOW!"
Fetal Eye View

In my judgment the first five pieces of the text are critical. Splurge with your best! They will determine if the reader goes further.

Most do not sit down and read a poetry book like they would a novel. They read it in bite-size pieces. That is why it is best to include a good entertaining variety of flavors in each bite. People also read the ones they like to others. If it is funny, philosophical, or compelling, the poetry will become a contagious habit and be returned to often. It makes the book useful beyond the initial read, for something other than a doorstop.

In addition to placing my poetry by my ABC method, I usually have my books loosely sectioned into categories like rodeo, veterinary, cow/calf, feedlot, horses, other animals, holidays, and universal, often generic themes. I don't necessarily make them into chapters.

After I have selected the order, I then pick the ones I would like illustrated. If I am using more than one artist, I carefully scatter them so everybody is represented in each section and we have good variation throughout the book.

This process is important in collection books, be they poems, anecdotes, cartoons, or photographs. It's where you get to put yourself in the position of the first-time reader. It is worth spending time on.

I think of my table of contents as a string of pearls, each poem a pearl. I use the same mental image when I am working on an audio collection or a live performance. In my speeches I mix and match extensively, depending on time allotted, my audience, the season, what they've heard before, and what new pearls I have to offer.

My incentive, be it for a book, CD, television special, book signing, or public appearance, is to entertain the audience, to give them their money's worth. And in the case of this book, to pass along business and life experiences that have helped me as an author and entertainer.

Lesson #62: If you are serious about publishing your own book, you, personally, have to be involved in putting your manuscript together. Grandpa Tommy said, "The best way to do something is to start it. . . . Drive the first nail."

Preparing a manuscript is your first nail. How many pages? Size of book? Illustrated? In color? Chapters? Title? Cover? Foreword? Introduction? Glossary? Font?

Make an exploratory trip to a bookstore. Keep an open mind. You should have a vague idea of how many pages your book will be. Look at the books on the shelf. Pick them up. Compare the heft of different sizes. Inspect how they are made, feel the type of paper, check positioning of illustrations if any, are they black and white, in color, are there photographs, is it sewn, glued, stapled, hardcover, softcover, color dust jacket, type and size of print, chapter page or title page?

Should it be 5 x 7 or 8½ x 11? Is there a foreword? A table of contents? An index? An introduction?

Design the book in your mind. This is the one time you can let it soar! Later, when you begin taking printing estimates, you may have to compromise. Some of the features of a book may have intrinsic value, like high-priced paper or end sheets. Others may have a direct effect on sales: color cover, inside illustrations, foreword by somebody famous. Other factors increase real value, like hardcover, size, color inside, but cost more.

When we design our books, we make lots of choices. One of the most important to me is the cover.

Lesson #63: A visual kiss is as good as a car wreck to slow traffic! A great cover is worth a thousand words . . . even if they rhyme.

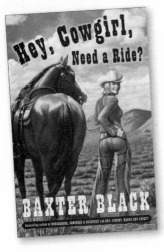

Need I say more? Look at the covers on all the magazines you can find. In the cowboy poetry world, horse magazines, cowboy magazines, farm magazines, art magazines, mailers from agricultural suppliers, other cowboy poetry books, and specialty catalogues. Line them up. Compare them to each other. Which fades? Which jumps out at you?

Do the same at a bookstore. Do the same at the vegetable displays at your Safeway. Walk up and down the aisles. Take your daughter with you for a second opinion. Squint. Walk by. Carry your ID in case you are mistaken for a burglar casing the joint! Discuss why one draws your attention even when you can't read the title or author's name.

Think about shapes, colors, and words on book spines, covers, signs, lettuce, and tomatoes. A sure bet for covers that attract attention are women and horses. Even if the only color you can afford is beige, at least put it on the cover.

Lesson #64: Regarding illustrations in your book: 80 percent of the population processes their information visually. Cowboy poetry is meant to be seen as well as heard!

I always use illustrations. My logic is this: If they come in the bookstore asking for my book by name, the illustrations would not be necessary. But for the other 99 percent who are just browsing in the humor or poetry section, they will first be attracted to the cover or the spine. They will flip it over to the back cover to see a picture of the author and read the blurbs. Then they will open to the inside front cover to see what the book is about. And last but not least, they will flip through the pages.

If it is all just writing, like the typical novel, they've seen all they need to make their decision without reading a sentence of content and will probably put it back on the shelf. But if they see clever illustrations, or beautiful drawings during the flip, they will actually stop and look at the picture and, if the drawing is compelling enough, they will glance to the opposite page of writing and read the first line of your poem.

Which pointedly demonstrates the value of the first line of your poem. But we are not discussing how to write poetry in this book, just how to get yours a broader market.

I always put the illustration on the right-hand side because that is the side a browser looks at first. Remember, I am trying to get them to stop flipping pages and "take a visit," as they say on the web page.

It is not necessary to have every poem illustrated. I personally lean toward more than less simply because it makes poetry eminently more readable. Reading through a collection of poems is not easy. Poetry is meant to be read or recited aloud . . . performed. Merely scanning or speed reading poetry loses the point. Much of the writing skill cannot be appreciated.

I recommend those who buy poetry books to read them aloud, even if you're alone, or at least move your lips.

Most of my books have not used inside color. I gain personal pleasure from the books where I did use it, but I do so sparingly.

Inside color illustrations are a definite luxury compared to a color cover, which in itself is well worth the money.

Advances in printing technology continue to make the use of color inside and out more affordable. These improvements are good for cowboy poets but have caused an explosion in the market of color photography books.

The length of your book depends on the quantity of content and how it is placed.

The use of illustrations can affect the number of pages in the book. They can be used as borders, half pages, full pages, or decorations. The arrangement of your poems can also influence the number of total pages. If each poem is allotted its own page, title, and/or illustration, it will require more paper than if you run them together like a novel. The more pages in your book, the higher your cost.

Lesson #65: The title is important, and size really does matter to attract attention when enticing a possible buyer.

The Last of the Mohicans, Lonesome Dove, Genesis, Rocky III, Presumed Innocent, Atlas Shrugged, Batman Returns, Rascal Flatts. What if they had used the name *A Trip To Cape Cod* for the movie title instead of *Jaws*? Or *Escape from the Nazis* in place of *The Sound of Music*?

Titles of books hold great power, even in the hands of an unknown author. Who wrote *Appliance Repair for Dummies, How to Make a Million Dollars without Leaving your Home,* or *The Chocolate Diet*?

A book title should give the prospective reader a clue what the book is about, e.g., *Implant Training in Foals* by Robert Miller DVM, *Cowboy Poems* by J. B. Allen, or *World Treasury of Mushrooms in Color* by Bernard Dupre.

Even if the author is not well known, book titles like *Murder Comes First*, *Kids Say the Darndest Things!*, or *Love Is Eternal* can be mentally categorized by a browser and examined or, of course, passed by.

Self-help books, for businesspeople or for those seeking mental, physical, or emotional inspiration, are frequently written by former CEOs, psychologists, and retired sports personalities with known identities. Or they have catchy titles: *The Seven Habits of Highly Effective People*, *Lessons from the Hive*, or *Don't Just Do Something, Sit There!: New Maxims to Refresh and Enrich Your Life*.

If the author is well-known, the title has less need to attract attention. James Michener, Janet Evanovich, and Elmer Kelton have enthusiastic followers who routinely buy their books.

Political attack books pummeling politicians and written by prominent pundits stir passionate partisans to purchase.

All these illustrations point out that the title of the book can have great influence on a buyer. These examples are universal. If you are a poet, cowboy or otherwise, you will be fishing in a smaller pond, and you know your audience. You may be known well enough within your audience to make the first connection simply by having your name on the cover. If so, you may take more liberties with the title.

I have some name recognition in the agricultural community, but my only connection to the urban world has been through National Public Radio. Therefore, on the cover of my Crown books, we routinely identify me as "Baxter Black, cowboy poet and former large animal veterinarian from NPR." On the cover of my self-published books we qualify it by stating "cowboy poetry by . . ."

You can see from the titles I have chosen for my books listed at the beginning of this book that I lean heavily on the language of the cowboy world I live in. I also attempt to make them catchy or funny. It is fun to be introduced before a program as the author of *Croutons on a Cowpie, Vol. 2* or *Hey, Cowboy, Wanna Get Lucky?*

If you have a poem that is one of your standouts and fans might recognize it, use the poem title for the title of the book. If you have a colloquialism, a nickname, an odd horse or dog, or a colorful, catchy phrase that is unique to you, use it. If you're not sure, ask your friends to suggest names for your book. In the end you can always title it Cowboy Poetry by Buffalo Bob.

Size matters, but bigger is not always better. I have learned to take into account the retailer's space when designing my books. Look at the typical size of bookshelves in a bookstore; 10½ inches is common.

I think of book sizes in terms of large, average, and small. The average-size book will more easily be displayed on the most common shelf size. It's what I call shooting at the center: a means of increasing the chance that your book will fit their shelf.

Books 5½ inches wide x 8½ inches tall are what I call average, large would be 8½ inches wide x 11 inches tall, small would be 4½ inches wide x 7½ inches tall. It is also possible to make the book wider than it is tall.

I have published all kinds, but I have learned to play the odds and shoot for the center.

Lesson #66: A foreword by somebody of celebrity interest to a reader can often make or break a sale. Pick your politicians with care! I would rather have a foreword by Wilford Brimley than by a democratic duck or a republican rabbit.

I have mixed opinions on the need for a foreword. The obvious benefit is to increase sales. It is an endorsement of the book, or more often of the author. If the writer of the foreword is known to the prospective buyer and said buyer has a positive image of the writer of the foreword, it should make the buyer more likely to look at and/or purchase it. The same logic can also apply to artists who illustrate your book.

However, if you invite someone to write the foreword who is unknown to the public, it has a different value. The foreword can help introduce the author, the story, or their background in a way that will increase the pleasure of the reader.

In 2002 Crown was editing my book *Horseshoes, Cowsocks & Duckfeet.* They asked if I was going to have a foreword. I said I had not planned on it. They suggested it would help and asked if I knew anybody famous.

I thought a minute, running through notables like Pinto Bennett, Tink McCauley, and Tuff Cooper, then I remembered, "I've corresponded with Dave Barry." "Dave Barry!" the editor said enthusiastically. "You think he might write your foreword? Contact him and find out!"

Dave Barry is a humor writer for the *Miami Herald* and is syndicated across the country. I had read his column off and on over the years. I, too, write a weekly column and am always on the lookout for inspiration, particularly if the story has an agricultural bent.

The Associated Press wrote a short article about Japanese teenagers sniffing fresh cow manure in plastic sacks. It was such a bizarre story it inspired me to write a humorous column about it.

The week after my column appeared, I noticed Dave Barry had written a column on the same subject! We had different takes on the idea, but both were funny. I sent him a copy of my column in care of the *Miami Herald*. A week or two later I received a printed card from him labeled "From the desk of Dave Barry." He had signed it, THANKS!

On the insistence of my editor, I wrote Mr. Barry a letter asking if he would be interested in writing a foreword for my Crown book. A few days later I received a card in the mail with *Miami Herald* on the return address. I opened it. Across the top was printed, "From the desk of Dave Barry." Below it he had signed, NO THANKS!

In the subsequent conversation with my editor, she kept insisting that I needed a foreword.

"Okay!" I said. "You want somebody famous, I'll get you somebody famous."

Baxter –

Many thanks.

Dave "Hopalong" Barry

DAVE BARRY   MIAMI HERALD   SEP 21 1991

The next day I e-mailed her a foreword for *Horseshoes, Cowsocks & Duckfeet* by Herman Melville!

It began, "Call me irresponsible . . ."

My editor called back. She didn't know exactly what question to ask. "Isn't he . . . How did you . . . Don't we . . . Where does . . . ?"

After two days of waffling, they finally agreed that I could use it, but they couldn't allow me to put "Foreword by Herman Melville" on the cover.

Herman Melville

I argued that it was funny and that was the point. Two days later I received a call from the president of Crown Publishing. He explained that there were serious issues and it was shaky ground.

My logic was simple: "We both know that he died in 1891."

"Of course," he said.

"And the copyright for *Duck-feet* is 2002," I said.

"Obviously," he said, "but the lawyers are worried . . ."

I said, "Tell the lawyers it's a joke."

To their credit they relented but qualified the cover by saying "With a Brand Spanking New Foreword by Herman Melville."

In the end the joke was on me. I discovered that most of the people who bought the book didn't have a clue who had written *Moby Dick*!

Lesson #67: My marketing philosophy is "Everyone's got a twenty!"

Pricing

The choices I make designing my books are to optimize the most marketable product I can get from a printer, that will allow me to retail a book for $24.95. This is a price at which big book chains will sell for $20.00 or thereabouts. I can sell the books on the road for $20 and not have to make change. Western stores and smaller bookstores can sell them full retail, and I, too, can still sell them on the Internet and at mail order for full retail.

Examples

$24.95 retail (45 percent mark up over wholesale)

$13.50 wholesale (usually a minimum order of six; sells directly to public)

$12.50 distributor (sells direct to smaller retailers at wholesale price with no minimum order and they make 10 percent)

$19.95 retail

$11.00 wholesale

$10.00 distributor

$12.00 retail

$6.60 wholesale

$6.00 distributor

In my case if I can make 40 percent to 50 percent of wholesale I'm comfortable. Therefore;

For the $24.95 retail book I can afford to pay $6.75 to $8.00 each.

For the $19.95 retail book I can afford to pay $5.50 to $6.60 each.

For the $12.00 retail book I can afford to pay $3.25 to $4.00 each.

The more you order, the cheaper they are. You need to include your artist compensation, computer typist, and editorial services in your cost if they apply.

So once I know how many I think I can sell in a reasonable period of time and how much money is in my printing budget, the printer can give me estimates for various book designs and features.

See, self-publishing is easy . . . all it takes is money!

In a Nutshell

This chapter is deep in the nuts and bolts of where to begin, how to proceed, and several obvious but often overlooked considerations when self-publishing. Although it is an accepted tenet that books about publishing books don't sell, I talked my editor into letting me include this chapter anyway.

I get many inquiries about writing, publishing, and marketing books. Almost always I wind up repeating much of what has been elaborated in this chapter. It is a how-to chapter.

I laid out details and directions, choices and thought processes that will get you in the self-publishing groove. It will give you a place to start. And, as Grandpa Tommy said, "The best way to do something is to start it. . . . drive the first nail."

Write the first chapter, write the first sentence, write the first word.

CHAPTER 11
Spectacular Belly Flops!

As you might guess, with all our marketing outrageously, or not, sometimes it just don't work. I'll tell you about a couple of "belly flops."

At one of our meetings in 2003, we came up with the idea of a newsletter. We were still behind in building a first-class website. I was a bit of a naysayer regarding the newsletter. It would be too work intensive. Publishing costs would be too high to justify the kind of first-class, all-color newsletter we all wanted. We agreed that it could be quarterly. I said even if the price was $20 a year and we sold 500 of them, that was only $10,000.

Granted, $10K is not to be sneezed at, but at the time I made that in one night doing a show. The newsletter was also going to require more writing, editing, and selling; plus it was labor intensive.

There was a lull at our marketing outrageously meeting, then one of the people who had read the book and kept the bookmark said, "Not $20 a year . . . $50 a year!"

The group's communal mouth dropped! Some laughed, then said it would never work. But it was suddenly clear to me that for us to publish a newsletter successfully and make it worth our while, we had to charge a lot. Fifty dollars times 500 subscribers is $25,000. That would definitely work!

And what if we enlisted 1,000 subscriptions? Rush Limbaugh had 25,000 on his list!

Suffice it to say, we put it into action. Its production demanded more attention than even I had imagined. We enlisted the help

A Cowful of Baxter Black

Volume 1   Quarterly Edition   June 2004

Baxter Loses Tooth

The Associated Poet

BENSON - A deciduous tooth Baxter Black has worn for over fifty years was finally pulled, kicking and screaming from its socket this spring the molar expressed disappointment, "I was there when he first tasted Miracle Whip! His Aunt Carol would make sandwiches using his favorite spread and cut them diagonally. I remember how he savored biting off the points and experiencing the tangy flavor.

"He, Baxter I mean, had been accustomed to the bland Hellman's mayonaise of his mother's choosing. She also insisted on cutting the sandwich straight across, thus leaving three sides of crust per half instead of two. A big deal to a six-year-old.

"As he grew older no permanent tooth came up under me. Dentists wanted to pull me then but his mom said 'Let's wait.'

"Then came Cervantes et Facabeche! That glorious poems, taste-bud bursting explosion of chile!

Although I was smaller than my neighboring tooth, I was still able to join the fist ball back into play now and then. Nobody complained.

"As a titan he discovered chewing tobacco. None of us were very happy about it. It was like living in a swamp but it apparently did us no harm.

See TOOTH page 4

Baxter Black and his molar on the day of extraction

A Cow Called Baxter? No, Bull!   Readers Corner / 10
■ See Baxter Live! Schedule of appearances / 2
■ Baxter's Prehistoric Column / 5
■ Cow Report / 12

A cowful is a great sufficiency.

page 1

of a competent person from outside to be the editor. She lived in another town, so much of it was done in cyberspace. And even though it turned into work, we all enjoyed making it and were proud of each quarterly issue. It was a quality piece of work.

We sent out two mailings, a fancy one describing the product and a second follow-up. Subscriptions began to trickle in. We maintained our optimism. It improved with every issue. We had a "hot potato" to re-subscribe. We offered a quarterly CD of that past three months' commercial radio programs. And yet at the end of eight issues, two years, we never collected more than 120 subscribers. Why did it go wrong?

Lesson #68: The newsletter went wrong because they didn't get their money's worth! That and my younger fans were drifting away from the habit of reading.

It was a twelve-page, full-color, filled-with-photos-new-material-and-personal information, 8 x 10 newsletter you could read in ten to fifteen minutes. The annual rate of $50.00 made each one cost $12.50. Even with the intangibles, added values thrown in like the CD of my radio programs, and the exclusive specials, it lacked value. It cost more than a 106-page magazine!

We sold it based on the buyer needing a gift for the dad who has everything and was a Baxter Black fan. It cost more per page or per word than any of my books!

Had we priced it lower, $20 or less, maybe it might have attracted more followers. But it was so labor-intensive I didn't have the business energy and crew to carry it for five years in hopes it might catch on.

Another factor was in play: the differing age groups in our fan base. By then most of our "techno-savvy" followers were tuning out of "printed paper" information and entertainment and into web-oriented information. Our older fans liked it, but apparently not enough of them!

It was grand fun to do, and although we all were relieved to have the "newsletter" burden off our shoulders, we go back and reread them fondly.

Although we have had one book out as a $50.00 limited edition product, most of my products have aligned themselves to my basic marketing philosophy, "Everybody's got a twenty!" They are often officially priced in our catalogue and for book-stores at $19.95, $23.95, $21.95, or $24.95, but when I sell them on the road, I sell them for $20 even because everyone's got a twenty! I often have locals selling my books and CDs after the show, so they don't need a change box. Unless, of course, the very first guy needs to break a $50 bill.

In 1997, looking for ways to encourage and entertain children of farmers, ranchers, and rural residents, my Canadian friend Larry Firmston and I came up with the concept of AgMan! As often happens in my thought processes, we laid down the whole program outline in fifteen minutes driving down the road. Implementing it took longer.

We needed a hero, a superpower, sidekicks, worthy foes, and someplace for our hero to work. Larry worked for United

Farmers of Alberta, Canada (UFA). They had a magazine and thirty stores around the province, and we thought AgMan could become their spokesman.

As it all morphed out over a period of time, I enlisted the talent of artist and brother Bob Black to flesh out the character. AgMan could transform himself into anything mechanical (combine, Shop-Vac, sphygmomanometer) with just the twist of his cap. Sincere, powerful, and always on the side of right. Think Dudley Do-Right!

His sidekicks were Farm Boy, a typical teenage farm kid who was computer literate, machinery obsessed, and agriculturally cognitive. Cool.

And Corn Silk, ag reporter, multimedia-savvy, sharp, articulate, knowledgeable, independent—the daring distaff.

As it had formed in my brain, it would be a four-panel, thirteen-week serial to run in the weekly rural and trade papers that carried my column. My formula involved presentation of the problem usually with the victims, introduction to the villain, AgMan to the rescue, villain wins first battle, AgMan makes comeback and defeats villain, and final panel along the lines of "Who was that masked man?"

I would rough out the story, actually writing the cut lines for each four-box weekly episode. Bro Bob and I would meet and spend several hours rewriting and feeling our way through each segment.

He would send me penciled-in completed thirteen-week episodes. I would go over it, and we would tweak the lines and maybe the rough drawing. We prepared three entire stories before I began to pitch it.

The episode titles included *The Locust Plague, The Hog Farm Disaster, The Mad Cow Smugglers, The Armadillo Mutants, Holstein Hijack,* and *Trojan Ostrich,* among others. Our villains were the typical bad guys in the lives of farmers and ranchers: locusts, animal rights terrorists, *National Enquirer* reporters, kudzu, rustlers, weather, and disease.

We made a full-color envelope. For my mailing to the newspapers we took my column mailing list, as well as several more possibilities that I personally selected from Gebbie Press. It was a large undertaking. It contained samples, ref-

erences, pitches, and an offer of the first six months free!

We followed this up in three weeks with a phone call. The first round of calls sent us reeling! Fully half of the editors said they didn't get the big green envelope with the character AgMan on the front and the giant star that said free! After an anguished week of calling, it turned out they thought it was an advertisement from a tractor company or just junk mail, so they tossed it without opening!

After the follow-up call we re-sent well over half the packages. Since it was from me, they thought it would be a funny cartoon panel like Jerry Palen or Ace Reid. When I started describing the four-panel ongoing saga, they were less receptive.

Some editors agreed to give it a try since they liked my column. Others agreed because it was free.

It was another mentally intensive and time-consuming project for me, and a strong commitment from the artist. He was always being pressed!

We reached as many as fifty papers carrying it up through the free trial period. Then they started dropping it and leveled out. The response was disappointing. As we approached the spring of the third year, I decided it was over. Bob finished drawing *The Terminator Pig*.

So there I sat with a beautiful set of eleven AgMan episodes. Surely I can still get something out of this. How to sell AgMan? A book! I'll collect them in a book! I was encouraged by cartoonists who had collected their work in paperbacks. Calvin and Hobbes plus Herman were two of my inspirations.

But the material I had was not enough to make a good book, so I set Bob on drawing an additional thirty-eight-page, 152 x 4-panel, full-length continuing episode called *The Typhoid Mary Trail Drive*!

That took another year, during which time we devised a scholastic workbook containing questions that might be addressed in each of the story's themes. We had it online! We would send the whole package to the VoAg FFA teachers.

They would buy thirty books for the classroom and get all the teacher's guides at no charge. I envisioned every Monday morning the teacher would put up one of the story lines on his screen.

Students could follow along in their books. The topics were all agricultural with a question-and-answer segment.

How could I go wrong?

Although there were a few vocational agricultural teachers who looked at it, I gave one free to every VoAg teacher in the state of Utah! It was as well received as Meatless Mondays in Montana!

We used the book as a Christmas product as well in 2003. I printed 10,000 copies. I think to date we have sold 2,300.

Where did I go wrong?

Projects like these cost more money than you can imagine. Not just the cost of the artwork, mailings, phone calls, and the enormous time it takes my crew and me. If I grossed $25,000 on the whole kaboodle, cartoon, workbooks, books sales, I'm guessing I'm out of pocket at least twice that!

Lesson #69: AgMan did not work because the concept was bad, I misjudged my audience, and I proved to be a dinosaur in a *Star Wars* world.

Bob Bose Bell, an experienced radio man, author, artist, and self-unemployed entrepreneur like me, told me right off the bat, a continuing story cartoon does not work anymore, especially if it's only once a week.

I found that out. Too much distraction. The reader can't remember the story line for just a short four-panel cartoon from week to week. I thought I was writing for a Greenhand freshman in high school, the first VoAg level. In the end it created more interest in much younger kids, so all the "educational" value was above them.

I also presumed that it would be a fun thing to do in a VoAg class just to start the week right. Obviously I'm not a teacher.

The book did not sell well as a separate item by mail order

or in bookstores because it was a cartoon book and thus ignored by adults, and it was written using a hero with Superman powers in a world of *Matrix* mentality.

The newsletter and AgMan are just examples of arrows fired into the sky that were fun but unprofitable.

Early on I produced and recorded a ninety-second radio commentary to be run three times a week called *Cowboys and Sourdough*. We enlisted the aid of a syndicator. It made a fair to middlin' success, but creating three programs a week, fifty-two weeks a year, consumed more time than I could devote to it. I produced it for two years and let it go.

I realized even then that, had I hired other writers to help me, I might have been able to keep producing it and maybe do even more, but that kind of pressure doesn't suit me. I prefer to write all my material even if it results in less output.

Lesson #70: The demands I make on my writing seem to be within my capability. I have consciously stayed within my limits.

The only writing I have done in collaboration with another person is songwriting. Some of my singing friends have rewritten my songs and had some modest success with them. I'm just flattered that anybody would sing one of my songs! I eventually was able to face a simple fact: I'm not a very good songwriter. It is an art unto itself and is not like poetry. I still enjoy trying but I don't have any serious expectations.

In 1983 I had made friends with a wonderful songwriter, Ed Bruce of "Mamas Don't Let Your Babies Grow Up to be Cowboys." He lived in Nashville. He got me on the *Ralph Emery Show*. It was exciting; I told my poems and they laughed. My songwriter friend and his wife took me out to dinner afterward. I was on cloud nine!

They toasted me, and she asked if there was anything else I would like. I said, "Yes. I'd like somebody famous to cut one of my songs."

She said, "Why is it that every poet thinks he's a songwriter, every songwriter thinks he can sing, every singer thinks he can act, and every actor thinks he's a poet! Why can't you be happy with what you've got?"

Lesson #71: Learn to be happy doing what you are good at.

Ten years after I dropped *Cowboys and Sourdough* I began producing my once-a-week radio commentary called *Baxter Black on Monday*. I can keep up with once-a-week commitments with ease.

Other less-than-spectacular ventures I have tried included making greeting cards, but I can't compete with Leaning Tree. I've still got boxes in my bodega. Another project I still have on life support is a little bedside book called *101 Goodnight Kisses*. I created romantic sayings that two lovers could read to each

101 GOODNIGHT KISSES

BY BAXTER BLACK

FORWARD BY JULIET

other. It was my hope that some of my foot-shufflin', snuff-dippin' cowboy friends might find it useful in courtship. It is beautifully illustrated by a terrific western artist.

A representative sample of the sayings would be, "If I could paint the sunset the color of my love for you, the angels would borrow it to wallpaper heaven." Or "If loving you was a handicap, I'd always have a place to park."

The only thing, I think, that would convince a publisher to take a look at the book would be if I could talk a famous couple into writing the foreword. I'm still workin' on it!

In a Nutshell

It is exciting each time we start a new project, be it a book, a mailing, a television filming, or a radio campaign! It's something new! Another opportunity to tickle the audience's fancy! What allows us to continue our outbursts of marketing outrageously is that we have several sources of income: the column, radio program, television, commercials, books, CDs, DVDs, and speaking jobs. This hodgepodge of enterprises allows me to experiment financially with other ventures. I've got a lot of eggs in a lot of baskets.

Lesson #72: Diversity is like fishin' with two rods; you've always got bait in the water!

Finally, it is difficult to plan for failure. It interferes with positive thinking. However, it is wise to be prepared in a general way. You must learn how to take a fall, be it physical, financial, or emotional. When you drop something, it breaks, be it a bank, a bone, or a heart.

I've experienced all three kinds of falls. They all take awhile to get over. My usual reaction is to roll. This method to get beyond trouble is not unique to me. Cattle feeders, the ultimate entrepreneurs, have as many lives as Larry King (or Geraldo Rivera, or Donald Trump). They crash and burn financially over and over and are miraculously reborn, acting as if nothing ever happened! They are like the Chicago Cubs at the beginning of each season. The slate is clean, their memories erased, and it's batter up!

Lesson #73: One of the secrets of life is knowing how to take a fall: physical, financial, or emotional. My usual reaction is to roll . . . and keep rolling till I can see daylight.

CHAPTER 12

Dead Horses and Moving On

This chapter could be titled "You gotta know when to quit." I have been married twice but have bought four wedding rings. Sometimes things just don't work out. It is the same with entrepreneurial projects.

Lesson #74: You've got to be able to recognize a dead horse when you see it and put down the reins.

There is no rulebook for people who make a living gambling on a long shot. You can bet on your idea or your project, throw your whole energy and cleverness into it, and sometimes it still can't stand on its own. It happens to all of us, in business, or in life, or in relationships, be it human, horse, or a sorry dog. You can't let those disappointments follow you around.

When I fell head over heels for Wedding Ring #3, I made a big point, out of respect, to inform the women whom I was simultaneously squiring around that I would not be calling on them when I was in their area. I was now engaged. I received a lot of phone messages, some profane, others relieved. I did receive a dozen roses with a card that read, "Please give these to the new bride with my condolences."

Truth is, I was not engaged, simply trying to do the right thing. The big night came, and I broke out the ring and popped the question. She gave the ring a pretty good goin'-over but then said, "I'm flattered but I've decided to marry the dentist."

I was living in an apartment building in south Denver and eating at the 7-Eleven. That night I wrecked my car, a second-hand 1974 Lincoln, and left it on the shoulder of I-270. The patrolman took me home.

My emotional state was undergoing a meltdown. I filled a pint bottle with tequila, put it in my belt, and lit out. It was 10:00 p.m. Sunday. I planned to walk until I tore that woman out of my heart. I recall wending my way through back alleys and mall parking lots in hopes of finding some robber or burglar to punch my lights out.

I finally arrived at the intersection of Evans and I-25. It must have been around 10:30 or 11:00 p.m. I climbed down the side of the overpass and walked out to the middle of I-25, an eight-lane freeway. Running down the middle of the freeway was a square rail about a foot wide standing on steel uprights four feet off the ground. I mounted the rail and began walking north, taking sips from the bottle and crying, singing, yelling, praying.

Occasionally I would stop, climb down off the rail, and pick up a hubcap or treasure of some kind. The walking was not so hard, but when the freeway went under an overpass, the rail clung to the pylons. I would have to turn my feet sideways and cling to the cement as I passed through.

By midnight I had run dry, so I decided to take the South Broadway off-ramp. Underneath, down below the freeway I saw a light. It beckoned me. It was a cantina. I walked up to the door and presented myself. I remember trying to tuck in my shirttail, but I had fallen several times and torn the buttons off. I had also scuffed myself a little and, I'm sure, presented a disheveled apparition carrying an armload of hubcaps, a license plate from South Dakota, and a Frisbee that said Coca-Cola on it.

It was a nice bar and fairly well-lighted, as I recall. A man and a woman seated at the bar turned to greet me. They took one look and immediately indicated my presence was unwelcome! They began shouting epithets. It turned out they were all motorcycle enthusiasts. I mistook them as friendly and strode right in.

I sidled up to a large fellow with a beard and a black leather jacket with chains dangling off it. He looked like Grizzly Adams. As I set down my armload, it made a pretty big racket on the bar. I leaned into him and asked with a wild-eyed glare, "Is this a cowboy bar?"

He hesitated, backed up, and said, "No. No, sir, it's not."

That was about the time a contingent of revelers lifted me horizontally and hefted me out the door. I remember saying, "Wait! I'll buy every cowboy in here a drink!" I suffered the indignity of them tossing my collection of hubcaps, license plate from South Dakota, and Frisbee after me onto the sidewalk.

In my misery I found myself sitting on the curb. A stranger walked out from the alley behind the bar and sat down beside me. He introduced himself as Mel. He asked if I had a cigarette. No, I said, but I've got some Copenhagen. He bummed a chew. I asked him if he had a cigarette. He said yes. I bummed a smoke.

We visited, and I told him my sad story and how I was going to walk until I tore this woman out of my heart. I can't remember if he teared up, but he excused himself and went back into the alley, returning with a six-pack of empty pop bottles. He counted them out, giving us each three.

I realized that these bottles represented his savings account. He was homeless and turned the empties in for cash. I was overwhelmed.

Suffice it to say, by the time my secretary picked me up on the street the next morning, I was as empty as a champagne bottle at a bachelor party. It took me a few days to get my act back together, but I never yearned for the dentist's girl from that night on.

Lesson #75: You can't win them all.

You need to be able to put it behind you. I can't say one learns from his mistakes every time, even if it's the smart thing to do. I've lost two "workin'-for-wages" veterinary jobs due to the companies changing hands. I've been divorced and started over with nothing but a piano and a deer head.

Lesson #76: Perseverance is the most valuable trait to have when the chips are down. Not being funny, smart, strong, or good-looking, just being able to get back on when you get bucked off.

Along the pathway to making your place in this world, you often find you are not competing on level ground. Nepotism, good looks, athletic ability, gift of gab, and wealth are typical factors that can rise up against you and diminish your chances.

I will remind you of something a friend of mine learned the hard way. He had applied to medical school with the highest GPA among the applicants from his university. To all our surprise he was rejected!

After his interview the acceptance board felt he was lacking in "social skills." They suggested he work for one year where he would gain greater insight into humanity, then reapply. For one year my friend worked in the geriatric ward in a big hospital. He reapplied, did his interview, and was accepted.

"What did you learn working with the old folks?" I asked. He said:

Lesson #77: Life is not fair.

How do you deal with life's unfair adversity?

I know many good hands in the rodeo world. People with the God-given physical gifts of balance and strength and the mental ability to focus and react. Some do well and some do not.

But I have seen those whose natural ability is less than some still do well in rodeo. They belong to the breed that has "no quit." They work harder, practice longer, sacrifice higher, study wider, and commit deeper than the competition, and they can win the big ones. We're talkin' about hangin' in there. The last man standing gets the prize.

But at the top of the heap is the naturally gifted person who has that quality of "no quit." In their prime they are unbeatable. The Ty Murrays, Jim Shoulders, Larry Mahans, Roy Coopers, Tom Fergusons, and Trevor Braziles are the A-Rods, the Tiger Woodses, and the Michael Jordans of the Rodeo Cowboy World.

I was invited to a branding on a big ranch in the Sandhills of Nebraska. I had had a speaking job in a nearby community and spent the night at the ranch. Next morning way before sunup we were saddled up and riding out to the branding corral. My host, the heir in this one-hundred-year-old ranching family, had mounted me on a tall, rangy, light-colored horse. As we rode along, the horse kept throwing his head. Finally I commented to my host that if he saw a piece of baler twine along the way I could make a tie-down and stop the horse's misbehavior. He glanced over at me and, putting me in my place, said, "We don't use 'em."

I worked on the ground for the first hour. They had three hundred calves to brand. Several good ropers were engaged in the corral, draggin' them to the fire. As can happen, they had a lull. The ropers were having trouble catching the calves. Bein' the wiseacre that I am, I shouted to the cowboys, "Ya want me to go over to the dairy and get a couple cowboys?"

I was pickin' on them, of course.

My host was standing beside me. "You want to rope?" he asked me.

"Sure," I said.

I climbed on that stargazer I had ridden over, shook out a loop, and headed into the calves. Several were crowded in a corner. Two happened to be standing side by side, four little hind legs lined up in a row. I tossed a heel loop in front of their hind legs, and both hopped forward right into my standing loop!

I pulled the slack, took a dally, and drug them both to the fire. As I rode by dragging this little package, one of the cowboys workin' on the ground looked up at me, mouth agape.

"That's how we do it where I'm from," I said.

Now anybody in their right mind would have stepped off his horse after that and left a monumental memory that would have been told around campfires for years to come. But, of course, I didn't quit. I missed the next five calves.

Lesson #79: If your stock goes up high enough to make you a nice profit, it's okay to sell.

In a Nutshell

This chapter admits that sometimes a project blows up on you or simply dies a slow death. In spite of all your clever thinking, fast talking, vast experience, and big heart, eventually you have to cash in your chips and walk away. Think the Tucker automobile, John Kerry's presidential ambitions, my fruitless quest to make AgMan a household name, my newsletter, and a long list of personal pursuits that never came to fruition.

I am content that I gave each serious venture my whole focus and investment, so win or lose, when I say that we tried, I know it's true. It's therapeutic. That way I no longer go to bed still trying to figure out how I can make it work.

Lesson #80: Success is not if you can beat the best there is; it is if you can be the best you are capable of being.

CHAPTER 13
Good Management Is Good Help and Enough of It!

How does one organize hecktosity, hectickness, and hectnality?

I have usually had anywhere from three to six people working for me, as in "coming to work every day," since becoming a self-unemployed businessman. The most visible position in our office is that of Secretary. It is capitalized, as in Secretary of Commerce, State, or Typing. Since 1981 I have had three women hold the position of Secretary of Baxter.

Your first contact with my office, be it telephone, e-mail, or business mail, will likely be my Secretary. She will help direct you to the person in the office who is best qualified to help you.

The attitude that we try to represent is, "How can we help you?" And mean it.

No grumpiness, no impatience, no apathy.

Her job has always been to sort my e-mail, type my columns and get them out, keep track of the column and radio lists, and book the speaking jobs.

I have routinely paid my Secretary a base plus commission, as long as you don't interfere with her bookings, which you will.

Lesson #81: A booking agent working on commission will always get you a higher speaking fee than you will get yourself (of course, they take part of it!).

It is more difficult to get the best price if you are having to do the actual negotiation yourself because most performers (artists, poets, singers) underprice their value. There is also the modesty gene, which prevents us from telling the customer how good we are.

I started very simply with my first Secretary back in that two-room apartment in Denver in the spring of 1982. I was still traveling for the animal health company and speaking on their behalf. But I had begun to take a few side jobs for pay in the $350 to $650 range. Friends of mine commented that I was underpriced. My Secretary and the secretary from the animal health company began coordinating my travels. I asked my Secretary to raise our speaking fee to $1,000 plus expenses. The new fee policy kicked in, and the first job she booked at $1,000 plus expenses paid off on July 30, 1982, for the North American Limousin Breeders Symposium in Wichita, Kansas.

In September of 1982 the animal health company merged with another and let me go. Although I began interviewing for another veterinary job, my Secretary continued to take the calls and book me. She was getting $1,000 for my fee the majority of the time. In the spring of 1983 I still had not taken a "real" veterinary job, in part because I was constantly on the road speaking.

My experience as the manager of a feed and animal health store in Idaho, as part of my veterinary responsibility, had given me faith in the power of financial incentive for salespeople.

I cautiously instituted a commission program for my Secretary, 10 percent of the fee over $1,000. I say cautiously because, as the talent, I doubted I was worth that much. Would I be able to give them their money's worth? Six months later our faith was borne out; September 22 for the Nebraska Pioneer Farm Banquet in Omaha and September 23 for the World Symposium on Crabbet Breeding (Arabian horses) in Denver, each grossed $1,500 plus expenses. And my Secretary had just made a hundred-dollar bill!

When I was the company veterinarian with the Simplot Livestock Company in the early '70s, I was also the general manager of the Western Stockman's Supply, Grain Mill, and Feed store. Two salesmen were on the payroll, good livestock men, well-liked, who represented the company around the community in a good light. There was a sales incentive already in force. It was complicated, based on the company profits semi-annually, and had not been paid for two years.

Although I had stretched my entrepreneurial marketing muscles in veterinary school, this was my first chance to take it to a new level. I remind you of John Basabe, the man I was working for, and the title of this book named after the style I learned from him. I didn't tell him I was eliminating the old Western Stockmen's Supply sales incentive. He didn't care about the details, he just wanted better sales.

I hired a new sales manager, an experienced salesman who was calling on me in my veterinary capacity. I then hired another gung-ho salesman. We divided the sales area into three territories. The two original salesmen were cowboys. They did not want to call on the dairy clientele that had begun to build in Idaho. The new man was glad to take them.

They all three had a base living wage, averaging about $750 a month. I revamped the sales incentive to make it simple. They received 1 percent of their gross sales monthly, graduating to greater percentages as they reached higher specified plateaus. Their gross sales were easily calculated and available for them to inspect anytime.

The new salesman left everybody in the dust! One month the sales manager complained that the new salesman was making more money than he was, and he was his boss! The first time the new salesman made a monthly commission of over $500 I sent him and his wife for a weekend holiday!

It was necessary to explain to the salaried employees, mostly the sales manager and accountant, that we were not paying him "too much money." For every $2 he made, we profited ten times that much!

I explained that we, the management, established the price of the product. We set it to make a profit. The salesman cannot change the price. Secondly, I pointed out, he works twelve hours a day, seven days a week. He badgers us for better deals; he is an advocate for his customers. They come first. He drives me crazy! And he makes the company money as well as himself, and that, my friend, was his incentive. Not company loyalty, or his company truck, or my praise. No, his incentive was that commission check!

My Secretary is analogous to the booking agent many professional speakers use through speaking agencies. There are occasions when we are approached by speaker agencies, usually at the request of the client. We are glad to work with them.

Most of my business life I have run a one-man show. Everybody working for my company is "selling" me. I am the Nascar, I am the product.

Lesson #82: Lines need to be drawn so that employees don't put themselves or you out on a limb.

Just a word about the job of my Secretary: She, more than anyone in the office, is put in the position of speaking on my behalf. The obvious responsibilities in her job description—such as booking the speaking jobs, scheduling transportation and lodging, managing the weekly column preparation and mailing (150 papers), organizing and sending out the radio program (120 stations), maintaining our daybooks and schedule calendar, and setting up interviews—can be well defined.

But when you put her in the position of sorting your e-mail and responding to the myriad requests that we receive, you need to give her guidelines for her sake. Each contact needs to be attended to properly, whether it involves requests for personal favors, charitable fund-raisers, certain poems, interviews, friends, fan mail, criticisms (some constructive), old classmates (real or imagined), book forewords, blurbs, unending poetry sent for comment, and assorted unclassifiable requests.

Lesson #83: Regarding your personal secretary (or booking agent or business manager), the hardest part of the relationship is trusting her judgment.

That comes with time. As any attentive boss realizes, after a while they can read your writing, your mood, and your mind.

It's when too much is taken for granted by both sides that you get sideways.

Lesson #84: Do not put off talking to your employees if you have a criticism that arises. The sooner, the better. Don't carry grudges.

Don't make it personal, even if the "infraction" was personal on her part.

Hiring new employees is fun but spooky. Have a formal employment sheet to fill out. Talk about her (or his) skills, what she likes and doesn't like.

I appreciate that human resources directors for government or big business are limited in the depth of their interview. But when you have five women in an office in a small town that requires sharing personal space, lunch, rides, families, and time, a key ingredient in the decision is whether she will fit in with the others. There is a seniority and territoriality involved. It might be a good idea to have the other employees interview the new prospect as well.

Another position in my office is that of product manager. We have sold close to one million pieces of product including books, CDs, videos, cassettes, DVDs, posters, cards, monogrammed knives, and who knows what else!

That involves inventory monitoring, reordering, packing, shipping, billing, and lots of orders to fill from the telephone, e-mail, and web page sources.

My product manager has grown her job description (and job security) by taking over the graphic arts responsibility for our product covers, mailers, and advertising design, and she oversees our web design.

She is now the producer of several of our latest books. We spent years sending our graphic artwork "out." Now it is "in house." This same person has a flair for studio work and now  does the majority of the electronic mastering for our CDs, radio programs, commercials, and promo spots. In a bigger business it would take several people to cover the tasks these two women handle.

Lesson #85: Having a small business does not preclude being able to do high-quality marketing.

For many years I was my own marketing and sales department. I personally dreamed up the "campaigns," and the people who worked for me tried to implement my wishes. Problem was, they already had their own responsibilities and my marketing plans stayed at the bottom of their priorities.

I would come home from the road with pockets full of notes on whom I wanted to call, what to write, research questions, and marketing plans. My brain was like a room full of butterflies. As soon as I walked in the door, each employee had some issue I had to deal with, not to mention an in-box full of letters and e-mail all needing my attention. Then I had my cows, my family, our church, and personal obligations that keep my life in perspective.

The analogy that described my situation best involves the gathering of moths that flutter around the porch light on summer evenings. The next morning when I walked out on the porch, there was a semicircle of dead moths directly beneath the light. Those were my ideas. Dead as those dead moths.

Shutterstock

Lesson #86: It takes more than the ability to write and rhyme to put a poem to work. It takes marketing.

In 2003 President George W. Bush engineered a tax cut to stimulate the economy after its crash following 9/11. I calculated how much of my money I would get to keep. With that in mind I gave my employees a nice trickle-down raise, gave some to charity, and created a position in my company for a marketing, promotion, and research person. That person would also help me develop a television program.

My marketing person works half-days, is good on the phone, can make cold calls, and is able to organize and coordinate the production, accounting, and promotion of the now successful television show on RFD-TV and U.S. Farm Report. In addition, when I come home with a pocketful of moths, we can do the digging to explore their possibilities.

We have several regular marketing campaigns of our own, including a public radio premium gift solicitation and a gold label mailer for new products. She also heads up many of the spontaneous mail or telephone "campaigns." I am still actively involved personally in the securing of sponsors for the radio and television programs, although my marketing person often does the follow-up.

Lesson #87: It is often helpful if the boss (or personality) makes the first call.

To prove this point, just look at all the CEOs who are pitching their own company. I mean, who wouldn't take a call from Bill Gates or Oprah Winfrey!

The function of "researcher" in my marketing person's job description applies most directly to writing the weekly column. Even if it is humorous, it often requires the verification of "facts." The Internet has streamlined the ability to get information. We depend on it heavily, and it is important that the information is correct.

We also respond to as much mail/e-mail as is possible. Being accessible to readers, listeners, watchers, fans, critics, and potential customers is something my company and I personally are still able to do. There is a stage in the ascension of a "celebrity" above which personal contact with fans becomes impossible. I think that most big stars miss the human reinforcement of the relationship, no matter how many books, CDs, or tennis shoe commercials they sell.

My wife's official position in the company is bookkeeper. Though, of course, she is much more. She and I have built the company with the help of a cast of thousands. Her official job description is bookkeeper, computer expert, proofreader, and company cook. Her unofficial responsibilities are as deep as the littlest detail, broad as our Internet reach, and essential as the pilot light in a nuclear reactor.

A word about working with your spouse. Notice I said working *with*. Even though on paper I may be listed as boss, in real life she can challenge my decisions with little fear of losing her job. There are books aplenty about working with your family and all the extra problems that ensue.

Lesson #88: Working with your spouse in your business is long-lived only if you can leave your work at the office.

We have a fifth in-the-office employee who assists with the accounting as well as shipping products during and after the fall mailing. She also has a great comic sense and has helped me as a sounding board when I am writing novels.

We have cows and the horses to punch 'em. I would not be able to have the "rancho" with all its corrals, outbuildings, cattle, equipment, gear, and horses without an outside man. He is also listed as "vaquero" on the credits of the RFD-TV program. Many of the television programs, video commercials, and photo interviews include livestock, and a "good hand" is necessary. He is also another man around to help me with the heavy lifting.

The company also pays for the skills of many, many others who do "day work," as we say in the cowboy business. Artists, graphic artists, photographers, directors, writers I can call for advice, technical web page editors, guest stars, studio geniuses to produce my CDs and do background music or sound effects, publishers, accountants to do our taxes, Bobby the Bug Man, dog trainers, concrete men, drywallers, plumbers, electricians, and on and on . . . although we shoe our own horses and I do the vet work.

Lesson #89: Do not overlook small towns if you have the advantage of choosing where you want to live.

Thomas Friedman pointed out in his book, *The World Is Flat*, that it is possible to sit at your kitchen table in Beech, South Dakota, and operate certain types of businesses all over the planet. My interpretation of his title is that a customer in Belarus can download one of my DVDs or CDs from our office in Benson, Arizona, and pay me. An advertising agency can send me a script by e-mail or read it to me over the phone. I can go into my studio and cut the commercial while they can listen to the recording live on a phone patch. Upon completion we can make a CD, transfer it to the computer, then we can turn it into an MP3 for the ad agency in San Francisco, London, or Belarus!

Shipping actual product (books, DVDs, or CDs) still requires manhandling. But with the rapid accommodation of the U.S. Post Office, FedEx, and UPS for business's need for faster service,

Shutterstock

it's often just a matter of short days for customers to receive their product.

The miraculous advances of satellite and wireless services continue to make obsolete such accepted essentials as ground line telephones, film photography, a compass, maps, and a backseat driver!

Even the smallest communities have access to most of these services.

In our years of business, we have had our offices near two towns that were 5,000 to 10,000 in population when we set up business. These were towns with one high school, one post office, one big grocery store, a local hardware store, feed store, and small-town government. Each was within an hour of a big city with an airport. We have never lacked for a local source of good employees.

I have had to give the pink slip to a few employees over my years of management responsibility.

Lesson #90: Letting someone go from your employ is never easy, but it's like having a baby; when the time has come, you just have to grit your teeth and do it.

You tell them in private at the end of the day. Have their last check ready if possible. Do it with dignity. Don't overexplain. If they cuss you or blow up, let 'em. Apologizing is necessary only if the dismissal is unavoidable.

As a grown man I've been employed by two livestock companies and an animal health company over a period of thirteen years. Two of the three companies let me go. The first because the feedlot changed hands, and the second because the animal health company merged with another and I was the new man. The third company departure was due to divorce and the need to quit the country.

Somehow life goes on. You suddenly become very focused on what is really important in your life. There's an old saying:

Lesson #91: "When you have enough to eat, you have lots of problems. When you don't have enough to eat, you have one problem." —Steve Radakovich

---

You rarely forget the people you've worked with whom you personally had to let go. In your heart you should wish them well.

In a Nutshell

I can say with confidence that bright, educated, talented, capable, and responsible people live in small towns as well as big cities. They also have been raised mostly in small towns, which is an advantage for me since a large portion of my business is done with people who are rural and work the land.

Throughout the book I have extolled the virtues of honesty, ethics, and compassion. Examples of how the application of The Code of the West, "doin' the right thing," works in my business abound, how "the way you treat others" affects your long-term business reputation.

I have pointed out that modern technology expands the limits of how you can do business and where you can locate your headquarters.

In veterinary school they had a class in ethics. I assume they teach it in law school as well. But I've always been bothered by it because I believe that if a person doesn't know the difference between right and wrong by the time he's sixteen years old, he's dang sure not going to learn it in college.

Lesson #92: Most small-town employees already understand the value system of cowboy ethics, which is a good thing. It's hard to teach someone the difference between right and wrong if it's never been part of their thought process.

CHAPTER 14

Managing Your Finances

This chapter will be short since at least half of the self-help books ever written are based on "managing your finances." They conclude with the basic same advice: "live within your means, don't risk what you can't afford to lose, enjoy life."

What I would like to present, particularly for those who are new at running your own business or just feel lost talking to your accountant, is the value of a financial statement—but not necessarily the one your accountant will review.

I will explain how to design a monthly financial statement that is useful in manning your business but first . . .

Lesson #93: CEO vs. CPA. It is a Love-Hate relationship not unlike cowboys vs. cows, reporters vs. politicians, or lawyers vs. criminals.

In each case both parties must have each other to survive. A cowboy without a cow becomes a decoration. Reporters and politicians have great animus because each wants to tell his own side of the story. Sometimes you will see a lawyer and his criminal outside the courtroom in deep discussion. Often you can't tell them apart. My best guide has always been, if he's a good lawyer, the criminal is always wearing a better suit!

My first experience with this contentious relationship of management vs. accounting was when I was made the general manager of a feed and animal health store, in addition to my veterinary responsibilities at Simplot Livestock. John Basabe saw no reason why I couldn't do it; besides, I was schooled in animal health products and nutrition.

The corporate headquarters that oversaw the livestock division of which the feed store was a part furnished an accountant. He was sent to "oversee the money."

The HQ assumed that the store manager (me) knew nothing about accounting. They were right, but I quickly learned that the HQ accountant knew nothing about management!

I asked to see the financial statement. They said it was not necessary. They would handle it and guide me. I got my back up and insisted. They showed it to me. It was a typical balance sheet with much financial speak: total fixed assets, accumulated depreciation, liabilities, retained earnings, total equity, and somehow in the end they fudged or "adjusted" total assets to equal total liabilities.

There exists a strong resemblance between computer nerds and accountants. There is no point in asking them to explain "how they do it." You must simply ignore their hieroglyphics and ask them for specific information that could be useful.

In my case my first task was to convince my assigned accountant that I didn't work for him or for the corporate HQ. He could send whatever kind of "official" statement he desired to HQ, but I needed a monthly report that would keep me on top of the business. He consented and over a period of months we designed one that worked and became the model for the one I use today in my business.

However, even today, my in-house accountant still sends the "official" statement to our accounting firm who then talks in sign language to the IRS ... I guess.

Lesson #94: Accounting people are like freemasons or rappers; they have their own secret language, rules, and handshake. Don't let it worry you. They don't understand what you're doing either.

To manage your business you need to know many things:

1. Total sales per year and per month categorized into profit centers.
2. Total expenses per year and per month categorized into product centers.
3. Cost of goods sold, expenses to operate, to promote, to market, and taxes.

With that information I will have what products sold the previous month and for how much, and what it cost me to operate. It shows year-to-date as well. I always look at the previous year's statement to compare.

You can make it as detailed as you want, but don't let the numbers scare you. Use them to figure out what's working and what isn't.

In addition I have a sheet attached showing money in the bank or invested and debt obligations. It tells me where I stand today.

The product manager keeps inventory on what is in stock, what's not moving, and what we need to reorder.

The following is a sample of the financial statement I use:

OCTOBER 2010

		MONTH		YTD		
Speaking	$0.00			$0.00		
	$0.00			$0.00		
		$0.00			$0.00	
Products						
Books				$0.00		
	$0.00			$0.00		
		$0.00			$0.00	
CD	$0.00			$0.00		
	$0.00			$0.00		
		$0.00			$0.00	
DVD	$0.00			$0.00		
	$0.00			$0.00		
		$0.00			$0.00	
Greeting Cards		$0.00			$0.00	
Cassettes/videos		$0.00			$0.00	
Miscellaneous				$0.00		
	$0.00			$0.00		
		$0.00			$0.00	
Products Gross Income			*$0.00*			*$0.00*
Media						
Columns	$0.00			$0.00		
	$0.00			$0.00		
		$0.00			$0.00	
Out There	$0.00			$0.00		
	$0.00			$0.00		
		$0.00			$0.00	
BBOM/radio	$0.00			$0.00		
	$0.00			$0.00		
		$0.00			$0.00	
Commercials		$0.00			$0.00	
Music		$0.00			$0.00	
Media Gross Income			*$0.00*			*$0.00*
Shipping		$0.00			$0.00	
Interest Earned		$0.00			$0.00	
		Net Income	$0.00			$0.00
EXPENSES						
Gross Salaries		$0.00			$0.00	
Operations		$0.00			$0.00	
Empl Share FICA		$0.00			$0.00	
Other Taxes		$0.00			$0.00	
	Expense Total	$0.00			$0.00	
	Net Profit		$0.00			$0.00
Estimated Taxes/Fed & State		$0.00			$0.00	
Personal Draw		$0.00			$0.00	
Miscellaneous Draw		$0.00			$0.00	
Personal Exp Total		$0.00			$0.00	
NET PROFIT AFTER TAX & PERS			$0.00			$0.00
MONTHLY GROSS	$0.00				$0.00	

One of the biggest criticisms accountants would have of my management-friendly financial statement is that I do not put the direct Cost of Goods Sold (how much it cost you to manufacture or purchase the actual book, CD, or DVD) against the actual sales per month.

It would be like charging my actual flight expenses against only those flights that show on that month's speaking income statement. However, most flights I book and pay for several weeks in advance. These would not show on my financial statement, but they sure will show on my Visa card! It is true, the accountants' method would let me know how much I was making on each product that sold and a running inventory, but it gives me no clue on how much money I spent or made that month.

I chose to be able to follow my cash flow and dollar sales on a monthly basis to stay on top of business. I like keeping my hand on the wheel. I manage my inventory based on separate updates, both physical and financial. By watching the year-to-date figures, I can still keep an eye on the big picture.

In a Nutshell

To run a business you need to have the knowledge, or hire the knowledge, to keep your books straight. But you're the captain of the ship. You need information to navigate the icebergs off your bow, not off your stern! Remember, accountants don't believe in miracles . . . but you do.

CHAPTER 15
Travelin'—Goin' Down the Road

If you are considering establishing a "national" business in a small town, travel expenses and convenience are a big factor. For many years we lived in a small town thirty miles north of Denver. Denver is a major airline hub. That is why I moved there from Idaho when I took the job with the national animal health company. While I was there, I morphed into a full-time entertainer. Denver was the perfect airport for my business to thrive.

Lesson #95: In the entertainment business, if you don't show up, you don't get paid!

The person hiring you is not very sympathetic to your tale of woe: The flight was delayed, I had a sore throat, my cousin died, I wrecked the car on the way to the airport, I got mixed up, I got held up, I got pulled over, there were hijackers on the plane! "I don't care!" they retort, "We put your picture on a billboard, we sold five hundred tickets, we rented the hall, everybody was there . . . except you-know-who!"

In over 1,500 performances, I have cancelled four shows. The reasons were because of 9/11, my son being born, and I missed one because of weather. I assure the people calling, "I don't miss a job! You can count on it." I also have had one cancel on me the day before the show because I wouldn't sign their contract. Ironically, it was my alma mater, New Mexico State University!

Hubs like Atlanta, Dallas–Fort Worth, Salt Lake City, Denver, Minneapolis, Chicago, Washington D.C., Phoenix, New York City, Raleigh, or Los Angeles give you the best choice of flights when you finally get to the airport!

When I was flying out of Denver, I could reach many of my destinations in one flight. Denver flies direct to places like North Platte, Bismarck, Billings, Spokane, Birmingham, Boise, Casper, and Farmington, plus all the major hubs. If I had to connect to Athens, Georgia; York, Pennsylvania; Midland-Odessa, Texas; Pendleton, Oregon; San Luis Obispo, California; or Bowling Green, Kentucky, I would leave Denver on an early morning flight, change planes in Chicago or one of the major hubs, and make it to my final destination, say, Lansing, Michigan, in time to drive my rental car to the Hamilton Co-op an hour and a half away to do a show.

Lesson #97: There are people who live where they have to live to do what they want to do, and there are people who do what they have to do to live where they want to live.

When we moved to Arizona for family reasons, I knew I was going to lose the major flight-convenience advantage. Now I live an hour east of the Tucson airport off I-10. Tucson is a midsize airport that has virtually no close flights (except a jumper to Phoenix). It is what I think of as a feeder airport. However, it does have several direct flights to major hubs: Los Angeles, Salt Lake City, Denver, Seattle, Minneapolis, Chicago, Dallas–Fort Worth, Atlanta, Houston, and maybe even one to Dulles International! A person can connect from there and get closer to their destination.

I find that now, because of the move, I often go in a day early, or make the first leg of the flight to the major hub, spend the night in a hotel near the airport, catch the connecting flight the next morning, and easily reach the venue. I am sure many frequent flyers would think my precaution goes overboard.

But I am vectoring my trajectory to coincide with the trajectories of four hundred or six hundred or a thousand other travelers coming to my show who are going to be at a certain spot at a certain time. I don't have a lot of leeway. I take no chances.

Lesson #98: Arriving to the job early or on time is good business.

In my case, I am often familiar with the people inviting me. I can arrive early enough to be sociable, walk through the barns at the fairgrounds, tour the museum, or look at the president's cattle. It allows you to establish a more personal relationship with your hosts and the ticket buyers. They appreciate it, and they will remember you as a person, instead of just an entertainer.

That means it is your responsibility to have an alternative plan when your flight is delayed beyond the connecting flight, or is cancelled.

When I arrive at the Tucson airport for a 6:45 a.m. American Airlines flight to Oklahoma City through Dallas–Fort Worth, I have backup flights written in my daybook by my Secretary. I know that United has a flight through Denver that leaves at 8:00 a.m. and connects to my final destination. I may even have a third backup. These backup opportunities may disappear if you're standing in line waiting to complain.

Because of my promise, "I never miss a show," I have booked flights on many occasions on other airlines right there in the airport because if I waited in the "cancelled flight" line, my window of opportunity would be gone. A word of caution: It is usually expensive, but if that's what it takes to make it in time for the show, that's life. You get no gripes and no sympathy. It is very likely that you will have to eat part of the fee, but it's better than a no-show/no-pay.

Let me give you an example of the contortions I have put myself through to get where I'm going. On February 24, 2001, I was stuck in a storm in Chicago. The flight from Denver had arrived an hour late. The airport was a zoo! My flight to Springfield, Illinois, had been delayed. Luckily United Airlines had a commuter flight every hour to Springfield, where I was scheduled to speak that night at the Illinois Beef Expo. There were at least two other flights that had been delayed or cancelled ahead of mine, plus regular flights still scheduled every hour showing on the display board.

The weather continued to worsen. I knew I could rent a car and make the three-and-a-half-hour drive if I left soon enough. My problem was, if I left before they officially cancelled my flight, my return ticket for the next day would be cancelled.

"But it's obvious you're not going anywhere," I pleaded. "Nobody's flying in or out of here, and if I intend to make my show, I've got to leave now!"

They were obdurate. "Right now your flight is only delayed. If you leave before your flight is officially cancelled, the rest of your return ticket will be cancelled. That's the rules," they said.

"But the weatherman says the storm will continue through the night," I begged.

"He don't know the rules. He don't work for United," the ticket agent said. "He's just the weatherman."

I came to the conclusion that I would still be sitting in Chicago at 10:00 that night with my suitcase in my hand. If you don't show up, you don't get paid!

I rented a car, drove two hundred miles in sheets of pouring rain through the gray landscape of the soggy Illinois flatlands. I made it to the cavernous Orr Pavilion on the state fairgrounds with five minutes to spare! It was a great night! There were 1,250 in attendance; I sold 150 books and went to bed wired!

That night in the wee hours I was on the telephone with United. I explained my situation: one flight delayed, three cancelled, and one missed. "But," she said, "you left before your flight was cancelled."

I asked her how many United commuter flights from Chicago arrived in Springfield yesterday evening. "None," she said. "Didn't you see the rain? We can't fly when it's rainin' like that!"

I asked if I could buy a one-way return ticket. Sold out, she said.

I called my backup return flight, TWA through St. Louis as far as Denver, but it was already delayed because of the weather in Illinois. I then checked the Yellow Pages. It was now around 2:00 a.m. in my hotel room.

The urgency I felt was because I had a job that very next night in Tucson! I was looking for any airline that could get me close. Southwest Airlines had a flight out of St. Louis to Phoenix. Perfect, except, of course, I had to drive my rental car from Springfield to St. Louis, one hundred miles, pay the drop-off charge, catch the flight to Phoenix, then rent another car on my arrival, and drive one hundred miles more to Tucson.

Gracias a Dios, I made it to the Trail Dust Theater for the big show, and we entertained a sold-out crowd of five hundred. I sold thirty-nine books and CDs. Their catch-22 cost me another $733. Worth it? Maybe you should ask the audience.

Lesson #100: A reminder, just as with the radio program director, newspaper editor, and book publisher whose job is to keep you off the air and out of print, you cannot take the behavior of the airline ticket agents personally.

Once you concede that it doesn't matter who is at fault, it's easier to think your way out of the situation. Because, just like when they lose your luggage, you are the only one who really cares! Be prepared to handle your own emergencies.

Let me give you one other example of sliding through the maze of flying commercially. It was March 1, 1995, the day after the new Denver International Airport opened. It was snowy and there was a backup at the deicing station. My destination to Stavely, Alberta, Canada, was for a show sponsored by United Farmers of Alberta (UFA). The flight was booked on Delta Airlines to Salt Lake City, departing at 8:35 a.m. and arriving at 10:05 a.m. It connected to Delta FLT 1784 to Calgary, which was departing at 11:00 a.m. and arriving at 1:00 p.m.

My maiden flight out of the magnificent new DIA airport was delayed over an hour. By the time I arrived in Salt Lake City, my connecting flight to Calgary had long departed. I missed it by ten minutes. The airline counter people said they had another Calgary flight that departed at 8:00 p.m. that night. Not good enough. I kept focused as I led them through other possibilities: back to Denver to connect to Calgary? To Chicago? Minneapolis? Seattle? Toronto? Vancouver?

I could feel the panic creeping into my stomach. Surely there must be a way. On occasion I have booked a private plane in an emergency, but crossing the border and the distance required to travel on this trip were daunting.

I was pacing the concourse, dragging my hanging bag on a set of "wheelies" back and forth. The program that night in the Stavely, Alberta, Community Hall was a typical "Supper and a Do" that I've done many of in Canada. The bar opens at 6:00 p.m., dinner is from 7:00 to 8:00 p.m., then my show. Larry, with UFA, was planning to pick me up in his new minivan at the Calgary airport at 1:00 p.m., which had already passed!

Then, out of the clear blue, as they say, I walked by gate D5, and listed on its departure board behind the counter was a 3:45 p.m. flight to Edmonton! My heart leaped! I ran to the counter.

I explained my dilemma to the ticket agent. "But," she said, "why are you going to Edmonton when you want to go to Calgary and we have a flight to Calgary that leaves at 8:00 p.m.?"

First, I had to explain to her where Edmonton was, north of Calgary, 173 miles.

"It still doesn't make sense." She was not very geographically cognizant, and it was hard for her to picture it. I laid out the entire plan: They traded my Calgary ticket for one to Edmonton on this flight—yes, Virginia, there were seats available. I knew from experience there were regular commuter airline flights between Calgary and Edmonton on Canadian Air. The agent had trouble trying to book that commuter flight on a foreign airline. I told her not to worry. If she'd just get me to Edmonton by 5:00 p.m. I'd take care of the rest.

I called Larry, told him I was going to be late, but I'd be landing in Calgary on the commuter at 7:40 p.m. that night. He said, "Great! We can still make it. I'll call the folks in Stavely and have them eat slow!"

Stavely was an hour south of Calgary. I changed my clothes in the back of Larry's van as we sped south on Canada Highway 2, and we walked into the community hall at 9:05 p.m. They were havin' a party! One of the local cowgirl poets had filled in for me. She was relieved, she said, because she was running out of material. She was wonderful and saved the day! Even though I was late, the bar stayed open, the folks were in good spirits, and the anticipation was high! The show had sold out their four-hundred-seat venue, and I was pumped! Nothing like a day navigating your way through airports to get your blood moving!

Lesson #101: Tips on flying commercially:

1. Know where you are going geographically.
2. Book the early flight to your destination, not the tight connection, close-call one.

3. Get to the airport on time.
4. Have a backup plan.
5. Avoid checking bags.
6. On close connections get an aisle seat near the front.
7. Don't forget your ID and passport (for Canada and Mexico).
8. Learn to take big steps!

I have many friends who are private pilots. They love to fly and are good at it. Years ago I made a decision to play the odds. I'm not the least bit afraid of flying, big planes or little planes. I have averaged 120 to 180 flights a year for thirty years. I put my trust in the pilots, the planes, the mechanics, the FAA, and the folks in the control tower.

I realized early on that my odds of crashing diminish significantly if I fly with commercially licensed pilots. Although I receive many offers from my rancher pilot friends to pick me up at the nearest airport and take me to the venue, I always decline. I rent a car.

I have always booked my speaking jobs "plus expenses." We do all we can to keep the travel expense down. Book and buy tickets early, fly economy rates, rent midsize cars, always turn it in with a full gas tank, stay in modest hotels, and charge customers only room and taxes. I do not charge them for extras such as meals, taxi, parking, or tips.

If we get a price bargain on a flight, it is passed on to the customer. Remember, it's not how much you made, it's did they get their money's worth.

Because I am a frequent flier on as many as four airlines at one time, I often get to board first, get bumped to first class, and get special treatment. I appreciate their kindness. When I get buckled in my seat and we hear "wheels up," I either fall asleep or get out my pad of paper and start writing, or review in my head my next program.

When I'm dry of ideas on the airplane and my mind needs a break, I work on the hardest sudoku puzzles I can find. It often takes me months to finish one.

Lesson #102: Air travel is the cheapest, safest way to get somewhere. Don't expect them to treat you like a customer at Ruth's Chris Steakhouse!

It is doubtful I would be in the business I am in if it weren't for two presidents who came along just as I was making my entrepreneurial start. In 1978 President Jimmy Carter deregulated the airlines and made it a competitive business. Whereas before, the rates and routes were assigned by the government, i.e., regulated.

Shutterstock

When they were deregulated, supply and demand took over. The number of airlines blossomed, ticket prices declined, and flying became affordable for the masses. I was one of them. Suddenly my ticket price was not higher than my speaker's fee!

Then in 1983 President Ronald Reagan reduced and simplified my taxes. He reduced the maximum tax rate of 60 percent to 28 percent and eliminated all the loopholes. See, the richest never paid 60 percent anyway! The high tax rate was meant to encourage them to invest their money in long-term, tax-deferred businesses like railroad cars, grain, art, and condos. The high tax policy was great for big business, but for a small businessman like me who wasn't sophisticated enough to find the loopholes, it cut me off at the knees! I would be stuck paying the maximum tax rate!

In a nutshell, President Reagan's tax cut allowed me to keep my own money and invest my earnings in my own business. I was able to hire employees, print books, experiment, expand, and grow. I remind you, I was a poet, and nobody in their right mind would lend money to a poet!

In a Nutshell

I am frequently asked if I get tired of the traveling. The answer is no. Maybe it is because my destinations are so diverse and I am always going to see old friends, make new friends, or see new territory. Each program I plan for each new group is unique. I must divine what it takes to make them laugh. I compare it to a salesman going down the road rehearsing his verbal presentation for the next call, over and over. What can I do to interest them in what I have? They write and rewrite their sales pitch, editing and polishing as the scenery goes by.

It takes an understanding family to live with a traveling man. I'm gone most weekends. People have their banquets, bashes, and celebrations on Friday or Saturday. I make it to church on Sunday about one-fourth of the time. But I'm one of the few dads who can do show-and-tell for the third-grade class on Tuesday morning!

If you are an entertainer or salesperson and don't like to fly and/ or travel, you are going to have to work locally or count on having a short career. Even if it comes easy, it still takes a strong commitment to make a living on the road.

SECTION THREE

WHY I WAS ABLE TO LEARN:

By maintaining my inner values,

By trusting my intuitions,

And by developing a faith that transcends publicity.

CHAPTER 16

Doin' Business on a Handshake

Doin' business on a handshake . . . it's not for everybody. If you are uncomfortable taking someone's word, it's possible they might feel the same way, too. But it works for me because:

1. My first instinct is to trust people.
2. I make the bulk of my living in a world outside of show business, which places a high value on a man's word. It is his bond.
3. With the exception of Madison Avenue commitments, I have no agents, managers, or middlemen looking over my shoulder watching to make sure I don't give away their share.

My "speaking business," performances, live shows, appearances, however you choose to describe what I do, are booked by calling my office, talking and negotiating with my Secretary, then booking me.

We send out a speaker's information packet that contains the date, location, group, responsible party, and speaking fee.

Shutterstock

When it is returned with a signature, we consider the date booked. The paper is to clarify the expectations of both parties. Should a catastrophe occur such as 9/11, or a local or personal problem arise on their behalf that would preclude my performance, I would accept the cancellation without malice.

Were the reverse to happen, a personal tragedy on my part, I would do my best to help them attain a substitute and offer to rebook my appearance at no charge. And yes, I have done it.

Lesson #103: When your business depends on word of mouth, your reputation is your most valuable asset. Bend over backward to keep it good.

I have done over 1,500 shows. There has only been one occasion wherein I was not paid. It was November 1984, times were tough, the cattle business was bad, lots of farmers were strung out with their bankers. I was hired to perform at a bull sale for a purebred breeder on the western slope of Colorado. At the conclusion of the sale, as we all watched, the IRS marched into the tent, took all of his money, and left.

A week later I received a check for my services. It bounced. I redeposited it twice with the same result. I called the rancher who held the bull sale. He was too ashamed to talk to me on the phone. I explained to his wife that I felt bad for his tribulations, encouraged him to keep his head up, and if he ever got back on his feet, to pay me.

He never did. That was the only time in twenty-five-plus years that I was not paid. No one ever tried to beat me out of my fee. There are occasions when I have voluntarily taken a reduced fee if, in the end, the attendance didn't live up to our expectations. I guarantee that I won't let whoever hires me lose money on my show.

Lesson #104: It's not about how much you made, it's whether they got their money's worth.

I will also add that on a few occasions, maybe five in my lifetime, when the program exceeded everybody's expectations, I was voluntarily, generously paid a little bonus.

As I am illustrating, it is possible to live your life and operate your business based on a mutual trust. But I appreciate, from the horror stories and experiences of some of my performer friends who are booked out of Los Angeles, Nashville, and New York City, there often is a contentious relationship between booking agents and program producers. It's as if each is trying to beat each other out of something in spite of having a contract!

Here are two examples of how things get "cloudy."

I had booked a date for a summer show to appear with a musical group. When the lady who was in charge of booking the "talent" questioned why I didn't sign and return her contract, I explained my policy, "I don't sign contracts." She protested that the other group had sent her a three-page contract! I told her I understood, they have their way and I have mine. She reluctantly conceded and booked me anyway.

Two months before the scheduled program she called me in a panic. "You're still coming to the program, aren't you?"

"Of course," I said, "I told you I would. Why do you ask?"

"The other group called and cancelled!"

I said, "I thought you two had a contract?"

"We did, but in the fine print it said they could cancel within sixty days of the show if they get a better deal, so they did!"

This second incident demonstrates the mind-set of some folks in the entertainment business.

A performer called me personally and asked if I could fill in for him on a program the following week. He explained that he had received an offer to perform for another group, which would mean a lot to his career. The original group had agreed to let him out of his contract only if I would come in his place at the same price.

I allowed as how I could come as a favor to him and to the group. Then he added, "But it really doesn't matter if I break the contact. My agent said I could keep 'em tied up in court for years."

In the beginning of this chapter I pointed out that one of the factors that allows me to do business on a handshake was the world I circle in. By that I mean the farmer-rancher-rural community world.

Lesson #105: The cowboy way is not just a punch line. It is a code of conduct that boils down to "doin' the right thing."

Another example of doin' business on a handshake:

When I lived in Colorado, I was approached by an ad agency to make commercials for a supermarket chain. The commercials were to be original, written by me, and they required a new one each week. Since I was traveling heavily, to do the commercials would take a serious coordinated effort. They would furnish me the "special of the week"; i.e., grapes, hot dogs, melons, hamburger, pork chops, etc., by Monday each week.

I was to have the finished, written, and recorded commercial to them by courier (Brighton to Denver) by Wednesday. They would approve it or, if necessary, request corrections. I would have the final back to them on Thursday and it would be on the air in Colorado and Wyoming by Friday morning.

After we had worked out that it was feasible, they asked for a meeting. The ad agency rep and the supermarket regional marketing person came to our house.

I have always had several guidelines that affect my consent to do commercials:

1. I will do the recording in my studio at the house. The ad agency folks are always invited to come and watch or we can do a phone patch. The reason is efficiency. Time at home is a precious commodity for me. I can record it in a tenth of the time it would take if we had to go to their studio, where each one of the managers, ad agency writers, producers, directors, brothers-in-law, and twelve-year-old children would ask me to read it "once again" with more emphasis on the word "the," or suggest I "put a smile in my voice," or could I sound more like Mary Poppins?

2. Besides, it's cheaper if I do it in my studio! Plus, any visiting out-of-town ad agency reps could stay over after the recording and ski Aspen!

3. I don't use my name.

4. I don't do pharmaceutical or medical commercials that conflict with the ethical standards required of doctors of veterinary medicine.

As I explained these conditions to the guests, it was "so far, so good." Then I said, "Number five, I don't sign contracts."

They looked at each other, the ad agency and supermarket rep. I could imagine the contract that bound them to each other with all its doublespeak, suspicion, obfuscation, and loopholes.

"What do you mean?" they asked.

I explained, "I make the commercial. You approve it. You pay me."

"How can we trust you?" they asked.

"I'm telling you I'll do it," which was the only answer I could think of.

"What if we don't pay you?" they asked.

I said, "I'd find out what kind of people you are and I'd never do business with you again, and that would be worth the thousand dollars you'd have beat me out of."

After getting approval from their supervisors, they consented and we struck a deal. One week after I delivered the first weekly commercial, their check had not arrived. I called the ad agency rep and asked where my check was.

"Oh," he explained, "we have to submit it to the accounting department and it goes through the system."

It was necessary for me to explain to him that when we made the deal, he agreed to pay me within one week of receipt of the final commercial tape. He gave me his word. I believed him. He stammered.

I pointed out that I didn't shake hands with his supervisor, his mother, his banker, or his bookie, my deal was with him. And if I were in his shoes, I'd write a personal check, if that's what it took to uphold his word, and have it in my hands by tomorrow morning.

DISCLAIMER

In spite of my maybe overly righteous convictions, I grant that dishonest, disingenuous, devious, shyster, flimflam artists can often take advantage of trusting people. However, I will also point out that a contract seldom stops them. I concede these people are around and you can get burned. But I believe they are the minority, and I put my money where my faith is and give a person the benefit of the doubt.

Lesson #106: I'd rather have an honest man's word than a crooked man's signature. "Honor is what no man can give you and no man can take away." —*Rob Roy,* the movie

---

On the bright side, which is where I am able to do most of my business, I offer this uplifting example:

In 2000 we had been in Arizona for three years. We were planning to publish my third self-published hardback book called *A Cowful of Cowboy Poetry,* 216 pages, color illustrations, and retailing at $24.95.

It has always been our practice to buy American, and locally if possible. We decided to have our publishing done in Arizona. Arizona Lithographers in Tucson came highly recommended. We had many discussions with them about our needs and their capabilities, as well as pricing.

When I sat down face-to-face with the owner, I found out that he was a follower of my work and a fan of western art. He did a lot of prints and lithographs for western artists.

I placed an order for 25,000 books at approximately $5 per book, a total of $125,000. "Do you need any money up front?" I offered.

"Nope," he said, smiling, and shook my hand.

Who do you think gets my printing business?

Lesson #107: I'm in life for the long run. Treat people like you'd like to be treated and take care of your friends.

Of course, every business practice has exceptions. Our exception was the relationship we had with Crown Publishing, a division of Random House.

Not only did we sign contracts with them, we used an agent and hired a lawyer to read the contracts. At first take you would think the issues are so complicated that it would be necessary to have a contract to make it clear.

But no! It's just the opposite. The issues are clear, but business-as-usual demands they create such convoluted obfuscating legalese that I have to hire a lawyer to muddy the water on my behalf!

In my case, my agent was my only lifeline to avoid indentured servitude-for-life to the book publisher! Any singer who has a record contract in Nashville knows the feeling.

I'm saying this with no malice. It's just proof of how hard it is to win when you don't play by their rules. The agents know the rules, and they have guided me the whole way. They plugged me into the big time. They negotiated royalties and advances I would never have dreamed of!

When I got the first advance on my first Crown book, *Hey, Cowboy, Wanna Get Lucky!* I mentioned to my National Public Radio friend and author, Bob Edwards, how I was worried about selling enough books to cover the advance. He said,

---

Lesson #108: "If you ever sell enough books to cover your advance, you better get a new agent!"

Crown Publishing furnished me with a wonderful editor for *Hey, Cowboy.* She read it and sent me a three-page, single-spaced list of 105 suggestions for consideration. I admit, had anyone assailed my poetry that way I would have taken umbrage, but it was only a novel and I gratefully accepted her advice. I also rewrote and self-edited the original, removing profanity and content that was too risque. The book had been written at a time in my life when I had less respect for myself and my fellow man.

The editor told me there was nothing in the book that was too "bad" compared to most of the books she edited. In her world of "Madison Avenue progressives," I'm sure that is the case. But for my audience, the rural agricultural community, it is important and good business to respect family values and cowboy manners. She thought I was being silly.

Lesson #109: A writer or actor does not have to talk down or coarsen his or her own behavior or material to suit a movie director, agent, book editor, or critic if you know it disrespects your audience. "Resistance to temptation is the greatest measure of character." —Anonymous

---

Everyone sets their own standards, and you have to live with yourself. It is nice not to have to sell my books and tapes with a warning that they may not be suitable for kids, grandparents, and your Baptist aunt. It makes life easier.

I would like to comment on the situation of doing business with friends and relatives. I do banquets, write columns, record commercials, and publish books and CDs. One of the burdens of being related to me or being my friend is that people will ask you to intervene on their behalf to get "discounted or free" services or product, or that I review their book, or look at their poetry.

For instance, "I know you and Baxter are friends. Call and see if you can get him to come down here and do a fund-raiser for our worthy cause."

This puts my friend or relative in an awkward position. Under normal circumstances when I get a phone call or e-mail from them, it's a pleasure. When they are put in the middle, it changes the reason for the call and thus our relationship.

My first question to my friend is, "Is this a favor for you? If it is, just tell me and I'll do what I can to make it work. On the other hand if they asked you to call, and you're not personally involved, just give them my phone number and we'll treat it like business."

In a Nutshell

To sum up doin' business on a handshake, for most in the modern global world it is probably a bad business model. But I remind you that most normal inroads are not available to poets, so it has always been necessary for me to live and work outside the box.

From the beginning of being a self-unemployed entertainer, I have consciously done business as if I were in it for the long run. I have chosen to avoid the same venue two years in a row. That allows me to have new material, and I can stay fresher for years. I also judiciously avoid booking jobs in neighboring communities that would conflict with the attendance of either. The same with new newspapers for my column, radio stations for my program, and sponsors for my RFD-TV advertisers. I protect their exclusivity.

This is the opposite of the way Nashville, Hollywood, and New York seem to work. They book their talent as if they will never get invited back. Book all you can as soon as you can because the talent's drawing power will disappear as quick as lightning leaves the sky! I remember knowledgeable Nashville folks saying the life span of the average new singing star's career is five years. From the Horizon Award, to the Hit Parade's #1 hit, to opening for Baxter Black in Russell, Kansas. Vince Gill and the Dixie Chicks have opened for me on their trip to stardom.

Personally, it is always an honor to be invited to write book forewords, CD liner notes, blurbs, or do "freebie" speaking jobs for worthy causes. It is flattering. Most entertainers and celebrity types have many opportunities to accept these invitations. Speaking for myself, I am forced to decline the majority simply because of time. Yet every year I go back and look at my bookings and find 15 to 20 percent of my performances were done for expenses only.

It's all part of doin' business. Entrepreneurs, more than most, know the value of a good reputation whether you're a landscaper, a mechanic, or a cowboy poet. Which goes back to your integrity, the way you live your life, and the way you treat people.

In the real world character really matters.

CHAPTER 17
Controlling Your Life—
Big Decisions Like Turning Down
Johnny Carson

In the world of academic poetry, where poet laureates and Pulitzer Prize winners come from, they have poetry readings. Cowboy poetry is more like a Shakespearean play in the sense that cowboy poetry is memorized and performed. I suspect that had I been a clever cartoonist, saddle maker, horseshoer, horse trainer, sales rep, county agent, ag professor, or artificial insemination technician, I could still have become a successful poet. The key is that I am an entertainer. On the speaking circuit there are characters from all walks of life: dentists, MDs, former war heroes, economists, football stars, people who have had miraculous recoveries, ex-CEOs, criminals, and retired politicians.

The strongest factor driving the "speaking" business for me has been the ability to attract bookings without the necessity of having to actively solicit. The demand for my services has been there from the beginning. It has survived by word of mouth.

It is my blessing, like another person's perfect pitch, fast feet, curly hair, or Einsteinian intelligence. Do I take it for granted? Never.

If the invitations dried up, I would get an agent in a Fort Worth minute!

But, having that advantage, it has influenced the way I do other things. I have already discussed the need for agents when you need one. But in the fortuitous situation that you are able to book yourself, it also means you have to set your own prices, negotiate, follow through, do the bookwork, and collect the money. You have to be responsible.

Lesson #110: It has been said that artistic people are often poor businessmen. But not all are, and it should not be used as an excuse for your failure to achieve.

I have many friends, painters, poets, singers, songwriters, horse trainers, musicians, and actors, whose lives have borne that out. A good manager, a mother, publicist, agent, lawyer, and/or broker is a blessing to them. It leaves them time to create, which is what they do best, while their "entourage" watches after their business.

Being in steady demand has allowed me to make choices that affect the direction of my life. For instance, in January 1992 I made my last of six appearances on *The Tonight Show* with Johnny Carson. He asked me to be on one more time before he retired and went off the air March 1992. I accepted.

The Rodney King riot ensued and shut down Los Angeles television for one week. They called and apologized but they had to cancel me to substitute some of the major stars who had been bumped by the riot. I understood. Johnny liked my stuff and that was enough.

Mike August, an agent with Triad Artists, later acquired by William Morris, called my home in Colorado and wanted to discuss managing my career. I was flattered but I told him I thought I was doing okay. He was quite persistent, I resisted. "Can I come talk to you in person?" he asked. "Sure," I said. He asked when was the next time I would be appearing in California. April 24, in Turlock. "What comedy club?" he asked. I said I was the banquet speaker for the Central Valley Production Credit Association.

April 24, 1992, I entertained a crowd of seven hundred California farmers. They paid me $4,000 plus airfare. Following the show, I signed books and talked to every farmer in there who wanted to tell me a story. Waiting patiently, taking this all in, was Mike August. I remember looking at him and thinking, man, that's what dapper means! He looked like a character from *Who Framed Roger Rabbit?*

He and I sat at the back of the Assyrian American Civic Club in Turlock where the PCA banquet had been held. Employees were still cleaning up the tables.

He complimented me on my stories, although he said he didn't get them all, and my ability to "schmooze," he called it. Then he began his presentation: "Triad is the biggest agency in the world, the best! It represents all the major stars, could make you rich, make you famous!"

He called me a stand-up comedian. (Maybe he didn't notice they were poems either.) I asked, to what do stand-up comedians aspire?

"First," he said, "Johnny Carson!" I nodded. "Okay, I've done that."

"Then," he said, "your own sitcom!"

I had the fleeting vision of walking into the back of one of those huge studios every day, like the one where *The Tonight Show* was filmed, and working there for eight grueling hours. Then fighting the traffic back to my modest apartment and my life on concrete.

I gave Mike a fair opportunity and finally thanked him and declined to be represented by Triad. He asked if I was going to be on Jay Leno's show. I said, "Well, I've already talked to them, and they don't want anything left over from Johnny's show."

"Do you want to be? On his show, I mean," asked Mike. "Ya know Triad manages Jay!"

"Sure!"

"Call 'em tomorrow," he said.

Back home in Colorado the next day I called the talent person for *The Tonight Show* with Jay Leno.

"Great to hear from you!" she said. "Mike August called, said Triad might be representing you."

"Well," I said, "Mike and I talked but, ya know, I've got a family, a wonderful life doin' what I do best, making cowboys laugh, so I think I'll just keep bookin' myself, but I'd still be honored to be on Jay's show. I was on with him once when he was the substitute host for Johnny."

"You mean," she asked, "Triad is not going to represent you?"

"No, but, ya know, like I said I've—"

"Thanks," she said. "We'll get back to you."

End of story.

I am flattered to have been offered their idea of fame and success. But I declined. You may deduce that my story is a good example of "If you want to win their game, you have to play by their rules." True enough, but think about it, how many people that *did* play by their rules never appeared on *The Tonight Show*?

Lesson #111: Each person has the right to define their own concept of success.

The first time *The Tonight Show* called me was in fall 1983. I got off to an inauspicious start.

I had been in the Denver area a couple years and had been doing interviews on several local radio and television programs. I was funny. The phone rang one afternoon and I answered. The lady on the line said she had been given my name by a "Hollywood" person as a possible guest. She was with *The Tonight Show*, she said.

My speaking business was booming, I was traveling constantly, I had published a couple books, I had recently remarried; in other words, I was busy. I told her I'd be glad to be on her show if I could work it in, bein' as busy as I was and all. I assumed it was a local talk show.

Could I send her a sample of my work? I said, okay, I've got a cassette. Where should I send it? When my pencil got to the word *Burbank* it stopped dead in its capital BUR!

"Is this the Johnny Carson Show?" I asked.

"Yes," she said, "and you're not going to be on."

It is not my nature to be brusque or rude. I'm usually friendly. I've thought back and convinced myself that I was polite, but apparently not "grateful, thrilled, obsequious, or game-show-thrilled" enough. She wrote back and said I was too "cowy."

Lesson #112: Try to always have your best foot forward or sooner or later you'll step on your tongue!

In the next four years I badgered them incessantly. The Cowboy Poetry Gathering was invented in Elko, Nevada, in 1985. *The Tonight Show* called and asked if I was a cowboy. I said, "No, I'm a cowboy poet." Not good enough.

Finally in 1987 *The Tonight Show* called and said to me, "Are you ready?" I will put words in their mouth; they were asking had I learned my lesson? It had nothing to do with talent, it had to do with developing the right attitude. It was also a matter of me being outside of their business model.

You can see from this story how lucky we cowboy poets were to be able to perform on national television, the Johnny Carson show! I tell people that when the one-hundred-year-old woman, the talking dog, and the cowboy poets got on Johnny Carson, it was because we fell between the cracks!

I benefited enormously from the exposure. I owe it to those good folklorists and cowboys who invented the Cowboy Poetry Gathering concept. It was my good fortune at the time to be the only human on Earth who made his living as a "cowboy poet." The right place at the right time.

I have made questionable decisions, such as turning down Crown's offer to publish my poetry and declining Triad's offer to be my agent. One of the factors that influenced how I made those life-changing decisions was that I was a grown man. I had crashed and burned more than once along the way. I had already lived one great life as a veterinarian in the cattle business, and now I had grown comfortable as a cowboy entertainer.

My sweet mother was widowed early from a man she loved dearly. She knew the value of living in the present. One of her profound observations that was passed on to me says:

There are other examples wherein I have made decisions that to an outsider would have seemed bad career moves. One that fits in here is the fourth year that I had been on *The Tonight Show* with Johnny Carson. The talent coordinator, Jim McCauley, called and said that Johnny wanted to have me on more often. I declined. It was not well received! I asked to explain. "I am on every January to promote the Elko Cowboy Poetry Gathering. Then you replay it in June. Every time I turn around somebody is saying, 'Just saw you on the Johnny Carson show!'

"Do you remember Stephen Wright, that droll one-liner comedian from Boston?" I asked.

"Oh, yeah," said Jim, "I don't know how many times we had him on . . . brought him back the next week! He was hilarious!"

"I think so, too," I said. "But I heard him tell an interviewer in later years that when he walked off the stage after his last *Tonight Show* appearance, he did not have a single original piece of material left in his brain. Remember Freddy Prinze?"

"Yeah, that was sad."

I said, "Jim, television eats people like me alive! People who think up stuff! I come on your show once a year and give you the very best I have, then you replay it. How can I beat that?"

He was not pleased, but I stuck by my guns. "I don't think Johnny's ever had anybody turn down a chance to be on more often, but I'll tell him."

Months went by. Usually sometime in the fall they would call and we would pick a date in January that I would be invited. It allowed me to work around speaking jobs. He didn't call, and he didn't call. I still saved the date, but I also had to concede that I was not playing the game by their rules. If they never called again, it would be the price that I paid.

They called after Christmas.

As time has gone by I have made other choices that some would judge unwise, or bad for business. One involved the invitation to write the foreword for a book. I had seen promos for it before the publisher called. It appeared to be one of those projects that I would be proud to be a part of.

The publisher and I exchanged correspondence. I was still not committing simply because of time constraints. She sent samples. The photography was grand. The narrative was well written. I was convinced and called to tell her I would be honored to write the foreword.

She was very pleased. I had been the photographer's first choice. We discussed how important the book was, the dignity it lent to its subjects, and the respect it showed for their values. Then, out of the clear blue she lapsed into profanity.

It was like she stuck a tack in my forehead! I babbled that I had to go, and we hung up.

I have mentioned that I have done enough business dealing with what I affectionately call the "Madison Avenue Pit Crew" that her colorful language was not new to me. But it has always made me uncomfortable. I realized that I didn't want to add one more person to my life whose phone calls I would dread. It didn't make me mad, just resolved. I called her back within ten minutes and told her I was disappointed but I had to renege on my offer.

She was taken aback. I explained it wasn't the book, and then told her my reason. The conversation that followed was not pleasant. To this day it makes me sad. After publication the book won a distinguished award. Congratulations to them.

Lesson #114: There is a certain protocol in doing business with strangers. It involves a mutual respect. It's probably not a good idea to break wind, grab your crotch, or do your Chris Rock rant imitation until you know someone better.

Not long ago I received a call from a casting agency in New York City. The person calling explained that I had been recommended to audition for a part in a movie that was in the works. I recognized the name of the movie. I had read the book. It was from one of my favorite authors. I even recognized the names of the producers and the star. To boot, it was a western!

I have never been in a real movie. I do a lot of filming for television, doing commercials, public television specials, and my program on RFD-TV, but nothing on the big screen!

I admit I had some trepidation; not about if I had the time, but how it would be rated. I asked if she

Shutterstock

could send me the script to read before I agreed to audition. She did. I read it and realized that I would have to decline.

My reason to her was that I wouldn't be able to be in a movie, especially a western, that I couldn't take my kids to see. I might get my picture in a movie mag but, in my world, it would not help my reputation. I go to great lengths to hold my products, appearances, and persona up to certain reasonable standards.

The casting lady was very understanding. I offered that if they were ever doing a western that was PG, maybe I could be considered. I hung up with no regrets.

The movie won Best Picture at the Academy Awards.

Lesson #115: First trust your intuitions.

DISCLAIMER

I do not claim to be a goody-two-shoes. I have written some raucous poetry, I have hit my thumb with a hammer, and I watch some R-rated movies. In fact, there have been occasions when I have done things I regret. There often is no good way to apologize or repair the damage. One just has to move on. I wrote this for all those who have offended egregiously and are still packing the anguish. It is called:

Courtesy of Kevin Martini-Fuller

The Cowboy's Document of Contrition

WHEREAS the average cowboy is a person of good intentions, generous to a fault, and kind to women, children, and animals and, WHEREAS said cowboy is often in the right place at the wrong time and driven by an overdeveloped sense of chivalry, bravado, and / or tradition and, WHEREAS you may frequently find said cowboy entangled at the center of many a controversial, embarrassing, or blatantly stupid miscarriage of sanity;

This form is offered as a document in which said cowboy acknowledges his participation in some grievous social, marital, work-related, animal-inspired, or tequila-afflicted misbehavior.

(offender please circle one or more of these excuses:)

1. I freely admit that I lost control of
    a) My mouth
    b) My good dog
    c) The balloons full of beer I was juggling

2. I now realize that

    a) It was not as funny as I thought

    b) You didn't have fire (flood) insurance

    c) Weed eaters are not the proper way to slice cheesecake

3. It is true

    a) I didn't know your uncle had a pacemaker when I handed him the HotShot

    b) You should avoid microwaving paint gun balls

    c) Skeet shooting should be done outdoors

4. I will not be surprised that my hosts

    a) Really expected more mature behavior

    b) Have written me out of their will

    c) Have filed suit to recover the cost of repairing the bass boat I fired up in the yard and the gazebo I wiped out with it

5. What I want the offendee(s) to know, in my defense, is

    a) I am fully aware of the damage I have done to (our relationship, the landscaping, the parrot cage), and I humbly apologize.

    b) I messed up. I'm sorry I did. I didn't mean to wreck (your party, our date, your grandmother's Bowflex). Sometimes I get carried away, and if you give me one more chance, I promise I'll try to do better.

    c) I am unable to remember what happened, but if the DNA matches, I take full responsibility.

(Print Name Here) _____

In a Nutshell

The years after the Johnny Carson run included a book deal with Random House, a burgeoning presence on National Public Radio, a commercial radio program, steady increase in column subscribers, several specials on national public television, expanding my business into Canada, the increased public awareness of cowboy poetry, famous people like Calvin Trillin, Tom Daschle, Charles Krautheimer, Paul Harvey, and Sandra Day O'Conner quoting me, trying to be a better father, and a steady stream of speaking invitations, mostly from the public radio and agricultural community.

Courtesy of Gary Gaynor, Tucson Citizen

I have never been a visionary. I'm not introspective about my motives or emotions. I am satisfied that through Christ I know where I will spend eternity, but I usually think in terms of the next two or three weeks: the speaking jobs coming up, the column to be written, the television show shoot, the calves to be branded, the horse to be shod, and the birthday card to make.

My calendar reminds me where I will be for a year in advance. But I keep my mind on the business at hand. It's part of giving everyone their money's worth.

And it allows me to inadvertently "sniff the roses." People like me often forget to do that.

CHAPTER 18
Faith

Any successful entrepreneur needs to have a renewable faith. One that sustains your belief in the face of defeat and discouragement.

> *"You call for faith: I show you doubt, to prove that faith exists. The more of doubt, the stronger the faith, I say, if faith overcomes doubt."*
>
> ROBERT BROWNING, 1855

Faith and belief are interchangeable. They are the internal flame of the optimist, the entrepreneur, and the devout. I have adopted from biblical teaching that faith can be strengthened. If you act positive, the more positive your outlook becomes.

Lesson #116: The more you practice your faith, the stronger it will grow.

I apply this principle in my relationship with God and to my business as well.

When I began writing my column in 1980, one of the first precautions that arose was how I would handle writer's block. I made a conscious decision early on that I would not have writer's block. I would maintain the faith that inspiration would come.

Over the years there have been days when inspiration sticks its head in the sand, but I refuse to worry or fret. I stand fast in my belief that it will come, and it always does.

That momentary worry, that little niggling doubt that creeps up the back of your neck will do you in. You must forcefully push it back! Get thee behind me, Worry! It becomes the pinhole crack in the dam that will eventually bring you down.

In the entertainment part of my life I do a live show. It is cowboy poetry. We cowboy poets do it from memory. Most of us have pages of poetry, reams of rhyme, filling our brains. In preparation for a show I decide on the program that I think will make them laugh, the string of pearls, poems and stories, that I will do in the presentation. It amazes some people that we do it from memory, but not actors. They, too, memorize their lines. Then we step onstage and the adrenaline kicks in!

HOME AT LAST

The first time I was asked to appear on *The Tonight Show* with Johnny Carson, I chose to do a poem entitled "The Vegetarian's Nightmare." It was a gentle satire on plants' rights and was inspired by the idea that plants feel pain. It was a poem I had done hundreds of times out loud. But that night . . . that night with twenty-five million people watching live, I began to quaver. That little niggling worry was creeping up my spine.

I was backstage walking up and down the hallways, saying my poem over and over to myself. One of the network staff saw me and asked if something was wrong. I told her I was worried about forgetting my poem.

"Well, duh," she said. "We have teleprompters, you know."

I replied with my best Sierra Madre response, "I don't need no stinkin' teleprompter!"

It took me back to my cowboy pride, into the cowboy mentality that is best demonstrated by this little joke: Hold your hand up in front of your face and repeat after me, "Betchya can't hit my hand before I move it!"

I think I do my best when there is something at risk, whether it was riding bulls, doing poetry, or making a cold call on a new customer. You demand more of yourself, and each step increases your faith.

I was on *The Tonight Show* several times, as were other cowboy poets. To my knowledge none of us ever used a teleprompter.

Lesson #117: Faith is a mental, emotional, and spiritual muscle that can be developed by exercising it regularly.

In business, faith can be demonstrated by:

a) Trusting that another person is good for his word.
b) Confidence that a partner or employee will do their part.
c) Shooting arrows into the sky to attract business.

In moral sensibilities, faith can be demonstrated by:

a) Relying on the promise of another person's love.
b) Believing there is some good in even the worst miscreant.
c) Intuition.

Dogs & Horses & The Rockies

In spiritual things, faith is demonstrated by:

a) Charitable giving.
b) Practicing forgiveness and mercy to all who offend.
c) Humility.

Having faith is a trait like believing or loving or fearing or having jealousy. It comes from deep inside a person. Others can listen to you and observe what you do or say and conclude what "they think" that you believe. But they don't know. Only you know the extent of your own faith, be it an altar call or writer's block.

In my case, I think my ability to have faith in my business practices derives from my basic, unquestioning faith in God. I have the power of being able to believe. It gives me security. It allows me to trust, to forgive, and to make business decisions for the right reasons that, at first glance, might not seem wise.

Though wealth can be shown in a monetary display, success is less clearly defined. It is the balance that you reach between what you make and what you spend, be it time or money. For all of us there is a responsibility to use our blessings to help others.

Lesson #118: When you can afford to be generous and are not, it marks you as a small person. That does not include being generous with other people's money; that only marks you as cheap.

Giving back is the joy and responsibility of us all. An anonymous kindness is one of the greatest gifts one can give. It will help you understand the oxymoron "'Tis better to give than to receive." And there is no limit!

"...go and sell what thou hast and give to the poor, and thou shall have treasure in Heaven..." Matthew 19:21

Be generous and it will be repaid a thousandfold.

In the book *Who Really Cares*, Arthur C. Brooks presents statistics that show that in the "Fund Raising for Charity" business the most reliable characteristic to seek in a potential donor is regular church attendance. It is the number one factor that indicates a person's willingness to donate both time and/or money for worthy causes.

My conclusion is that if you lack confidence, self-esteem, and the faith in your own ability to achieve, you must first learn how to believe. Start

with God. Once you open up your heart and mind to His miracles, you can begin to believe in yourself as well.

It is truly the Power behind the positive thinking.

In a Nutshell

*How does being generous, honest, compassionate, and reverent make
you a better businessman, salesman, marketer, or cowboy poet? It
depends on how you define "better." If better is defined by your wealth,
to the exclusion of all else, it is a very shallow praise.*

*I think it is better to be defined by how you used what you had, or
how you treated your customers, or your employees, or your contribu-
tion to the community or your commitment to aesthetics like the arts
and fishing. It is seen in farmers voluntarily maintaining wetlands,
schoolkids visiting the elderly, the scholarships you have given, show
lambs bought at the county fair, your memberships in civic groups, or
faith-based food banks, hurricane cleanups, or overseas missions. They
all contribute to how good a businessman you are.*

*I made the point that each person has to define their own idea
of success.*

*If you go to bed at night dreaming of how you are going to invent
the next wheel, or bake your best bread, or write the poem that's been
swimming in your mind all day, that is a good thing. It's the way
some of us are, and it's what we do. It defines entrepreneurs. We're not
even thinking about money. We have the faith that if we can make
the clock tick, in time, we will be rewarded.*

PERSONAL NOTE: *Even ten years ago I could not have written
this book this way. I'm beginning to get my priorities straight.*

THE END

INDEX